Piano • Vocal

THE BEST
BROADWAY
COMEDY SONGS

ISBN 978-1-4950-9792-8

7777 W. BLUEMOUND RD. P.O. BOX 13819 MILWAUKEE, WI 53213

THE BABY SONG

from I LOVE YOU, YOU'RE PERFECT, NOW CHANGE

Lyrics by JOE DiPIETRO
Music by JIMMY ROBERTS

poo. Can I stop this? God, I wish it, 'cause I sound just like a dip- shit!

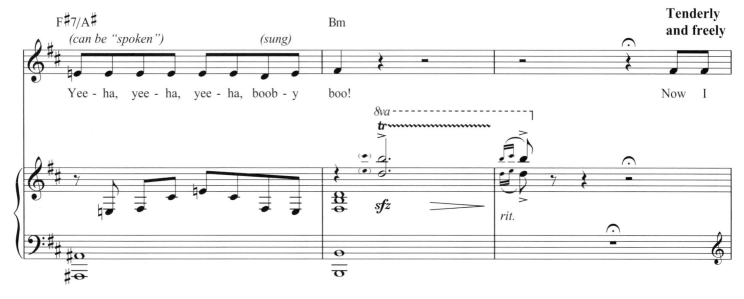

Yee - ha, yee - ha, yee - ha, boob - y boo! Now I

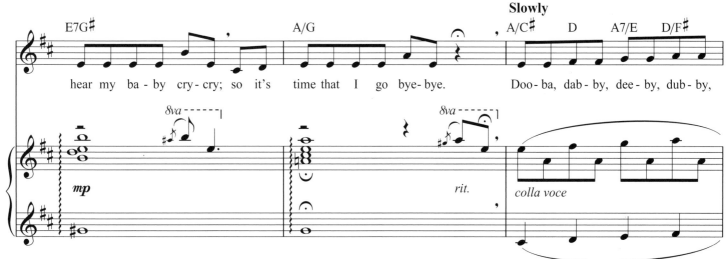

hear my ba - by cry - cry; so it's time that I go bye- bye. Doo - ba, dab - by, dee - by, dub - by,

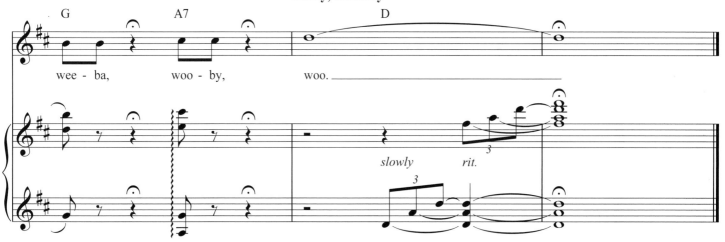

wee - ba, woo - by, woo.

COMEDY TONIGHT
from A FUNNY THING HAPPENED ON THE WAY TO THE FORUM

Music and Lyrics by
STEPHEN SONDHEIM

Lyrics:

Some-thing fa-mil-iar, Some-thing pe-cu-liar,
Some-thing con-vul-sive, Some-thing re-pul-sive,

Some-thing for ev-'ry-one— a com-e-dy to-night!
Some-thing for ev-'ry-one— a com-e-dy to-night!

Some-thing ap-peal-ing, Some-thing ap-pal-ling,
Some-thing es-thet-ic, Some-thing fre-net-ic,

An ensemble number in the show, this song has been adapted as a solo.

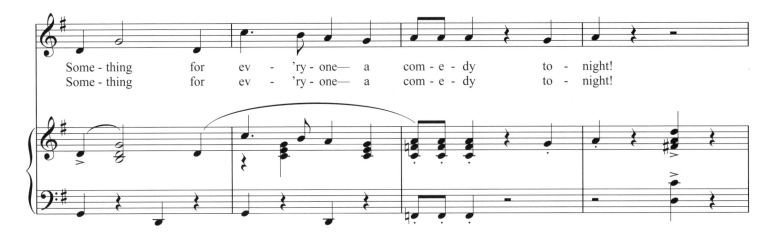

Some - thing for ev - 'ry - one— a com - e - dy to - night!
Some - thing for ev - 'ry - one— a com - e - dy to - night!

Noth - ing with kings, Noth - ing with crowns,
Noth - ing with gods, Noth - ing with fate.

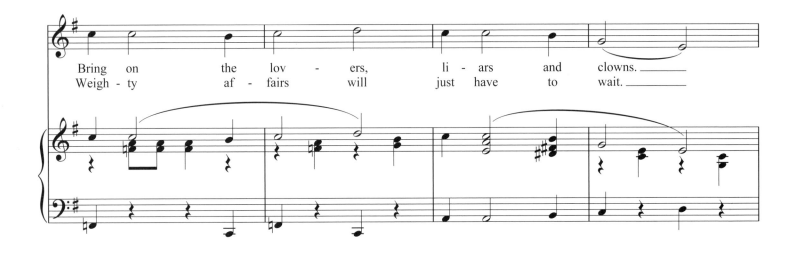

Bring on the lov - ers, li - ars and clowns. _____
Weigh - ty af - fairs will just have to wait. _____

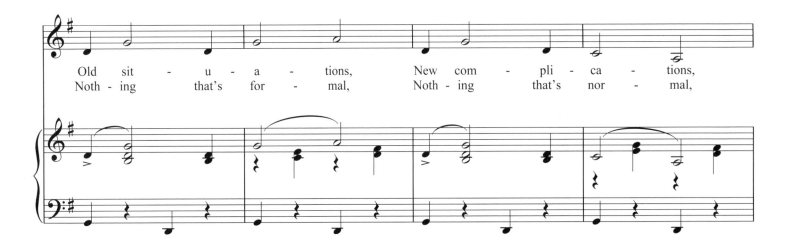

Old sit - u - a - tions, New com - pli - ca - tions,
Noth - ing that's for - mal, Noth - ing that's nor - mal,

Noth - ing por - ten - tous or po - lite. ___
No re - ci - ta - tions to re - cite! ___

Trag - e - dy to - mor - row, Com - e - dy to - night!
O - pen up the cur - tain—

Com - e - dy ___

___ to - night! ___

BEWITCHED

from PAL JOEY

Words by LORENZ HART
Music by RICHARD RODGERS

This is the original show lyric. Hart fashioned a standard lyric that appears most often in print, and can be found in other publications.

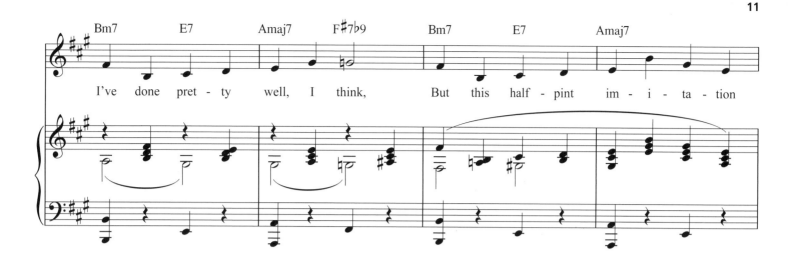

I've done pret - ty well, I think, But this half - pint im - i - ta - tion

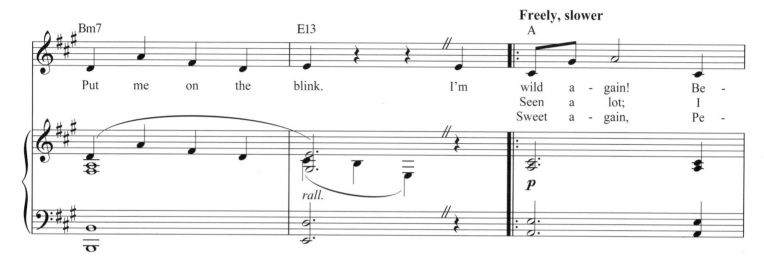

Put me on the blink. I'm

Freely, slower

wild a - gain! Be -
Seen a lot; I
Sweet a - gain, Pe -

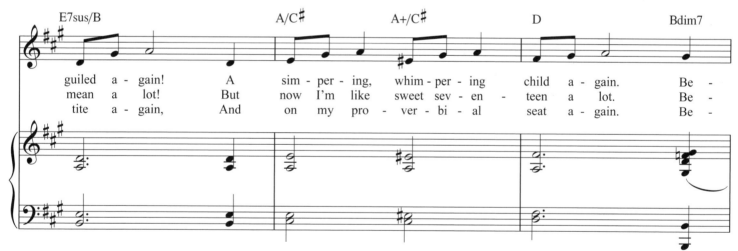

guiled a - gain! A sim - per - ing, whim - per - ing child a - gain. Be -
mean a lot! But now I'm like sweet sev - en - teen a lot. Be -
tite a - gain, And on my pro - ver - bi - al seat a - gain. Be -

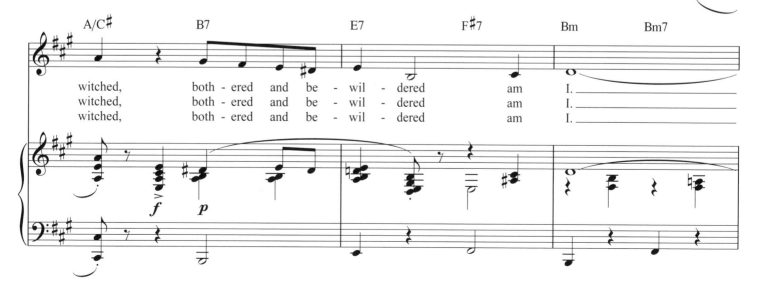

witched, both - ered and be - wil - dered am I.
witched, both - ered and be - wil - dered am I.
witched, both - ered and be - wil - dered am I.

BRUSH UP YOUR SHAKESPEARE

from KISS ME, KATE

Words and Music by
COLE PORTER

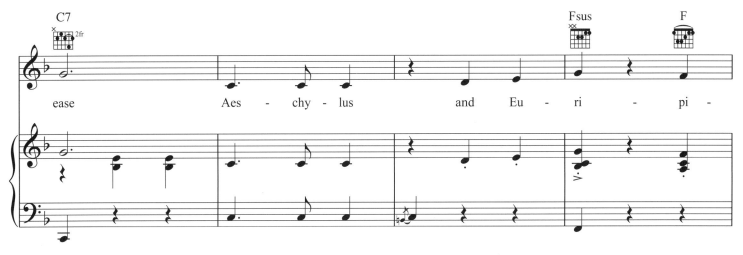

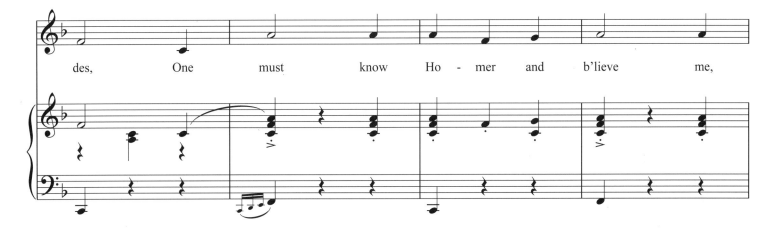

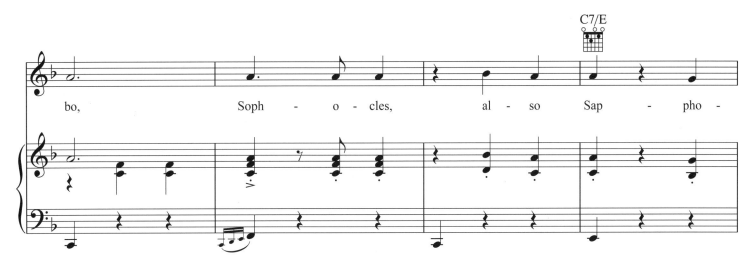

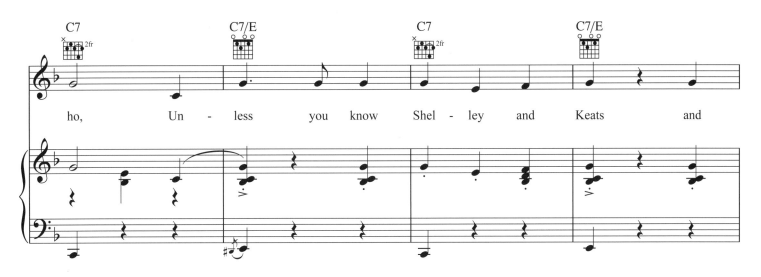

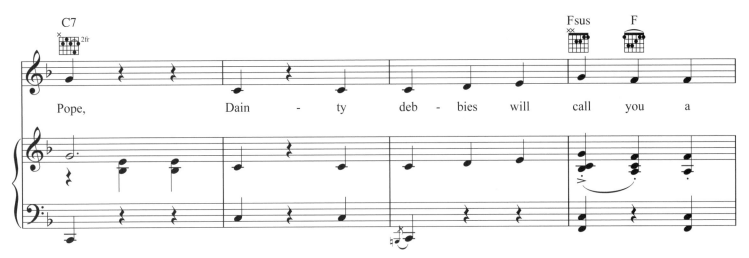

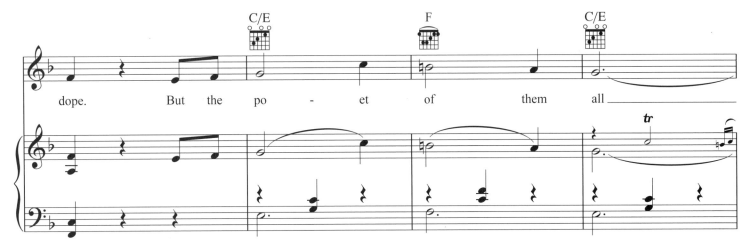

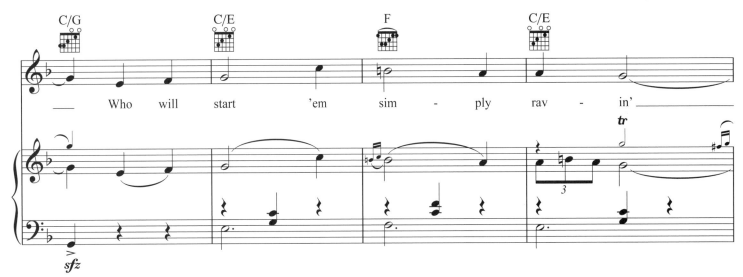

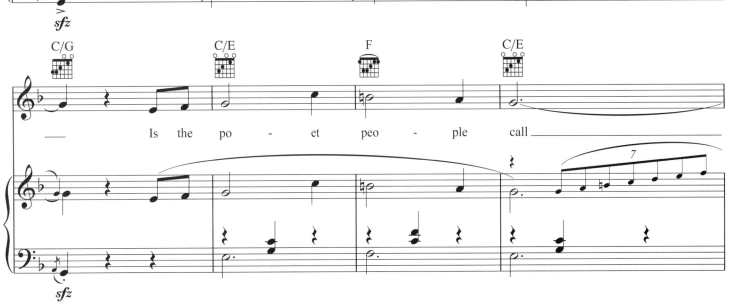

18

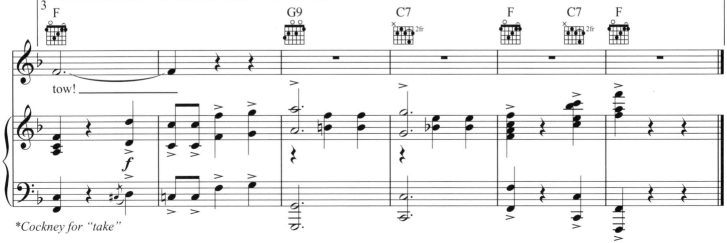

*Cockney for "take"

EVERYBODY OUGHT TO HAVE A MAID

from A FUNNY THING HAPPENED ON THE WAY TO THE FORUM

Music and Lyrics by
STEPHEN SONDHEIM

A duet in the show for Senex and Pseudolus, this song has been adapted as a solo.

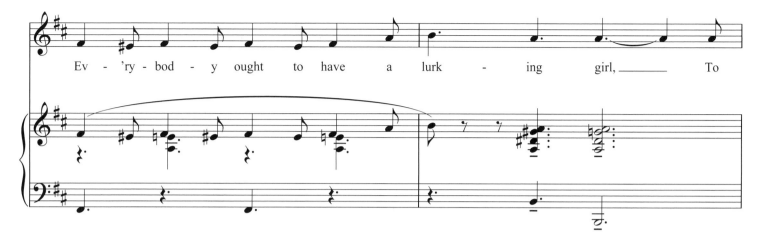

Ev - 'ry - bod - y ought to have a lurk - ing girl, _____ To

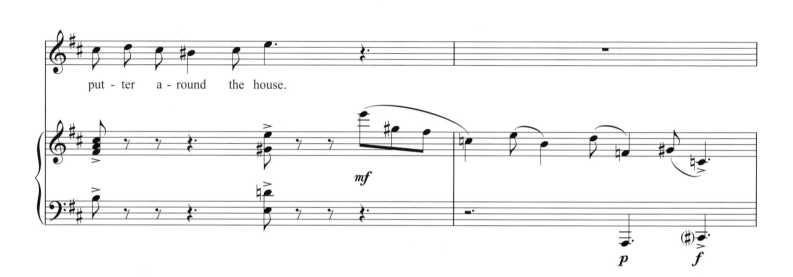

put - ter a - round the house.

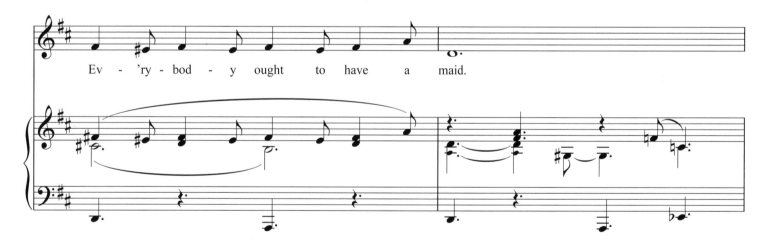

Ev - 'ry - bod - y ought to have a maid.

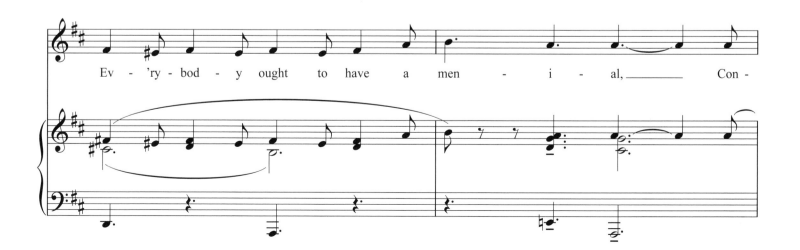

Ev - 'ry - bod - y ought to have a men - i - al, _____ Con -

sist - ent - ly _____ con - gen - i - al, _____ And qui - et - er than a

mouse. Oh! Oh!

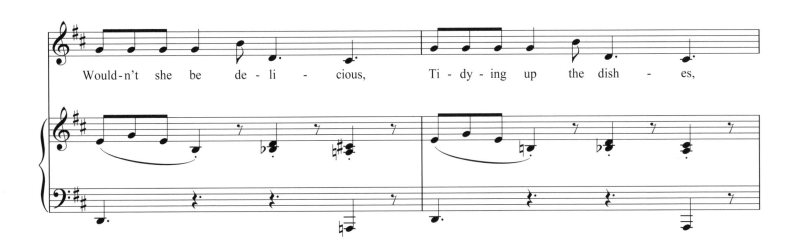

Would-n't she be de - li - cious, Ti - dy - ing up the dish - es,

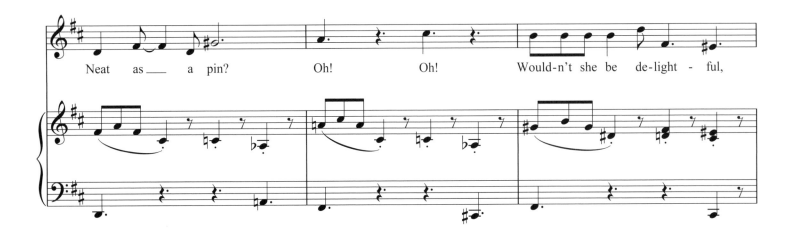

Neat as _____ a pin? Oh! Oh! Would-n't she be de-light - ful,

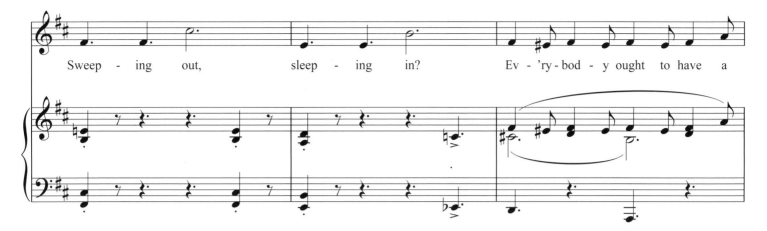

Sweep - ing out, sleep - ing in? Ev - 'ry-bod - y ought to have a

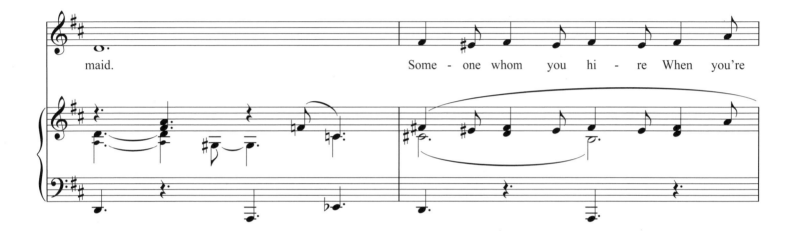

maid. Some - one whom you hi – re When you're

short of help ___ To of - fer you ___ the sort of help ___ You

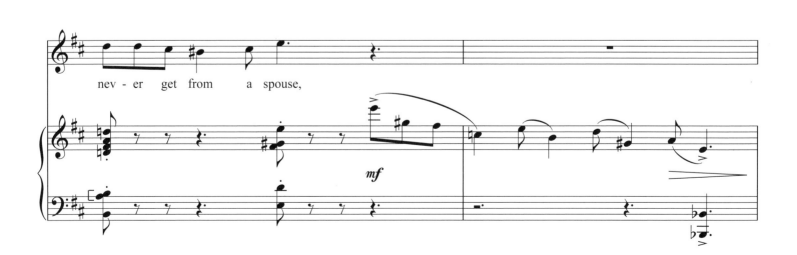

nev - er get from a spouse,

mf

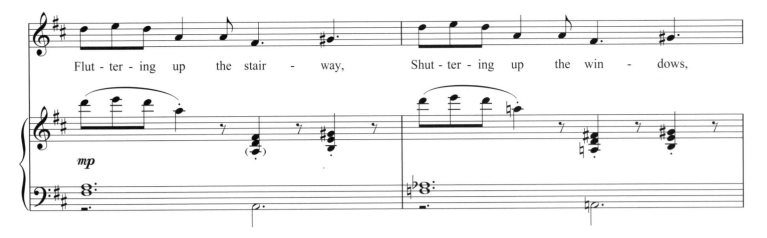

Flut - ter - ing up the stair - way, Shut - ter - ing up the win - dows,

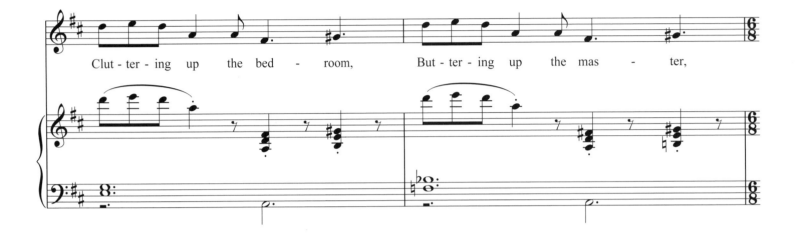

Clut - ter - ing up the bed - room, But - ter - ing up the mas - ter,

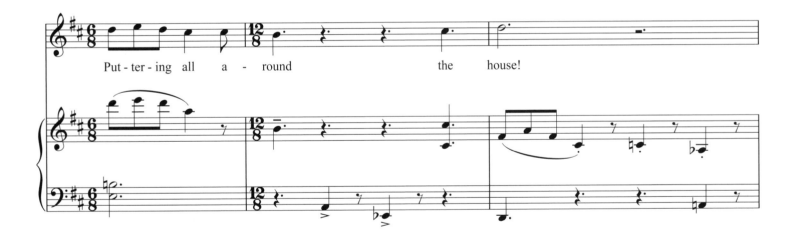

Put - ter - ing all a - round the house!

Oh! Oh! Would-n't she be de - li - cious,

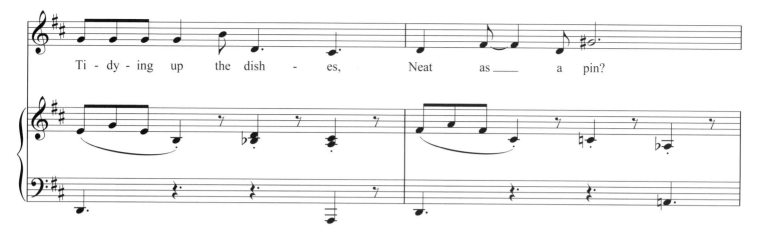

Ti - dy - ing up the dish - es, Neat as ____ a pin?

Oh! Oh! Would-n't she be de-light - ful, Sweep - ing out,

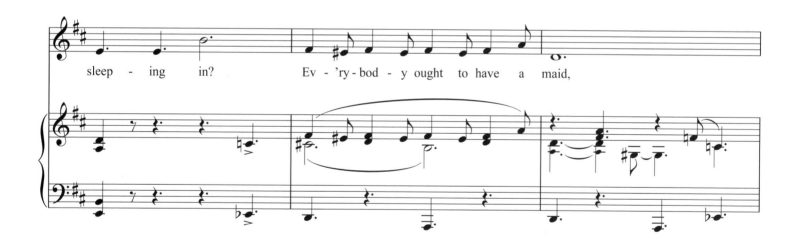

sleep - ing in? Ev - 'ry-bod - y ought to have a maid,

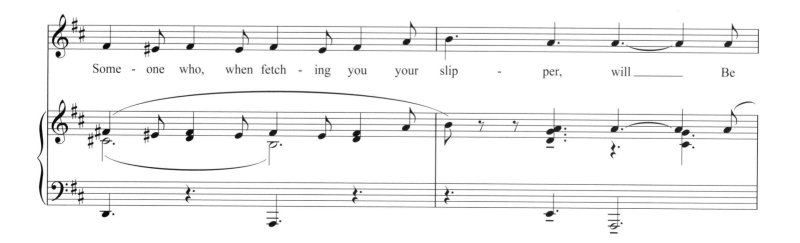

Some - one who, when fetch - ing you your slip - per, will ____ Be

win - some as _____ a whip - poor - will _____ and grace - ful as a grouse,

Skit - ter - ing down the hall - way, Flit - ter - ing through the par - lor,

Tit - ter - ing in the pan - try, Lit - ter - ing up the bed - room, Put - ter - ing all a - round _____

_____ the house! _____

GREAT BIG STUFF

from DIRTY ROTTEN SCOUNDRELS

Words and Music by
DAVID YAZBEK

Freddy is accompanied by ensemble, eliminated in this solo edition.

great big stuff! This is how ___ I got-ta live. Great big stuff! Uh - uh, no ___

___ al - ter - na - tive. Great big stuff! I want ___ my sil - ver spoon. Don't

need it right now, but I bet - ter get it soon.

I want a

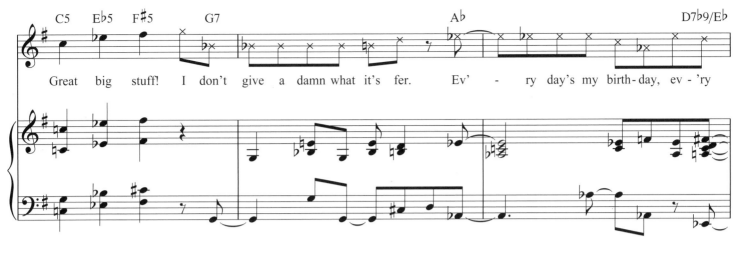

Great big stuff! I don't give a damn what it's fer. Ev' - ry day's my birth-day, ev -'ry

night is my bar mitz - ver! Hey! Hey!

(klezmer solos)

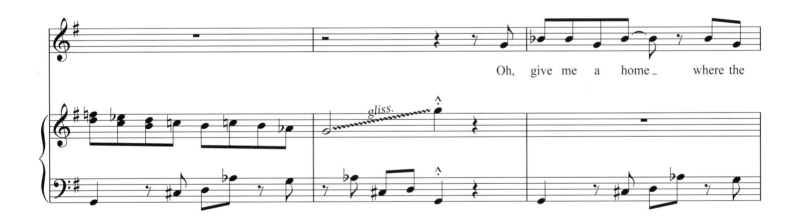

Oh, give me a home＿ where the

cen - ter-folds roam, Guc - ci - o - ne on the phone, he's got a par - ty go - ing on. And

Hef 'll have me o - ver to play some na - ked Twis - ter, blot - to in the grot - to with a

C5   Eb5   F#5   G7

play - mate and her sis - ter!   Great big stuff!   *(Spoken:) Rap stars 'll love me!*

C5   Eb5   F#5   G7   C5   Eb5   F#5   G7

Great big stuff!   *Get me a posse, A'ight?*   Great big stuff! Chil -

Ab   D7b9/Eb   D7   G7

- lin' in the cit - y, sit - tin' pret - ty in the Cad - dy with P. Dad - dy or Puff Did - dy or what -

This phrase, sung by ensemble in the show, can be sung one octave higher by Freddy from this point on, each time it occurs.

Great big stuff! Noth- ing crass or crap - py. Great big stuff! That would

make me ver - y hap - py. Great big stuff! Bring it on and make it snap - py!

(Spoken:) I want some really classy shit!

Like a mink track suit! *My own personal Zamboni!*

Lots of unnecessary surgery!

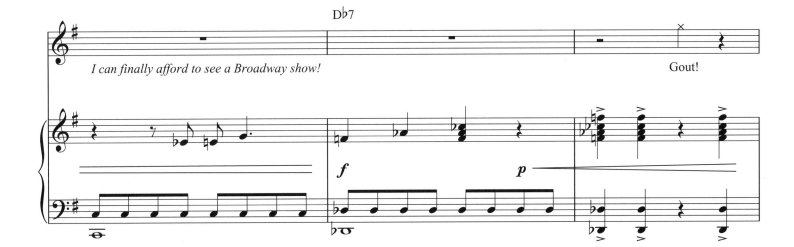

I can finally afford to see a Broadway show!

Gout!

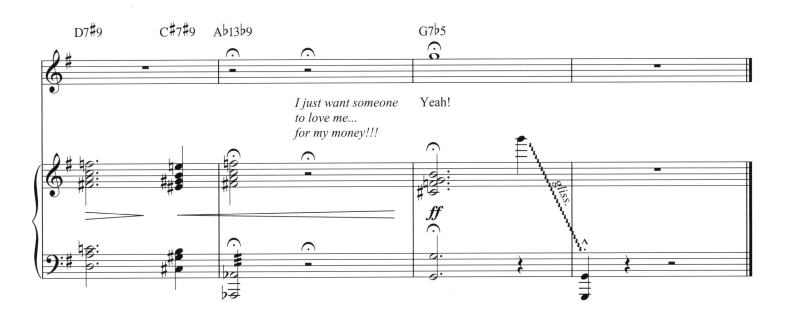

I just want someone
to love me...
for my money!!!

Yeah!

HABEN SIE GEHÖRT DAS DEUTSCHE BAND?
(Have You Ever Heard the German Band?)
from THE PRODUCERS

Music and Lyrics by
MEL BROOKS

bang, mit a boom, mit a bing bang bing bang boom!

Rus - sian folk - songs and French ooh - la - la _____

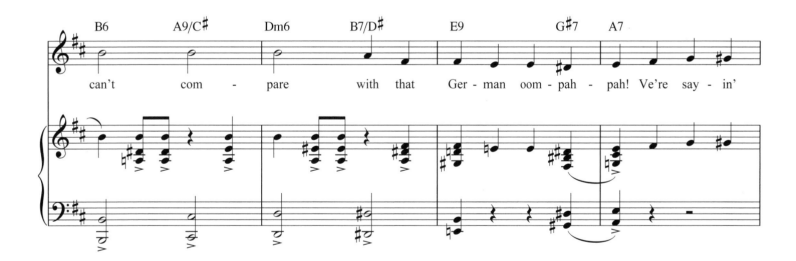

can't com - pare with that Ger - man oom - pah - pah! Ve're say - in'

Ha - ben Sie ge - hört das Deut - sche band? _____ Mit a

Pull back

Ha - ben Sie ge - hört das Deut - sche band? _____ Mit a

A tempo

zetz, mit a zap, mit a zing! _____ It's the

on - ly kind of mu - sic that ve huns, and our hon - eys love _ to

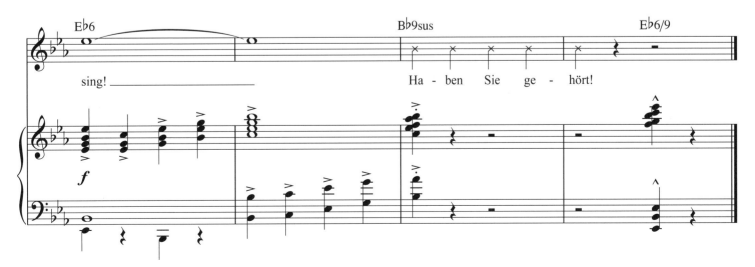

sing! _____ Ha - ben Sie ge - hört!

HARD TO BE THE BARD

from SOMETHING ROTTEN

Words and Music by WAYNE KIRKPATRICK
and KAREY KIRKPATRICK

SHAKESPEARE: *Honestly, I don't know how I do it.*
I mean, there's only so much of me that can go around.

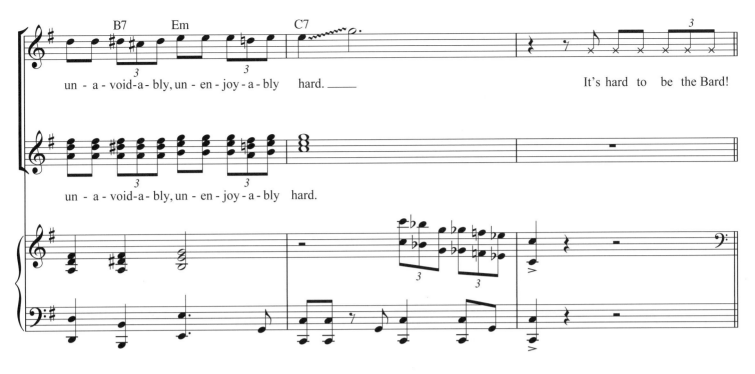

un - a - void-a - bly, un - en - joy-a - bly   hard. _____   It's hard to be the Bard!

un - a - void-a - bly, un - en - joy-a - bly   hard.

SHAKESPEARE: *I know writing made me famous,*
but being famous is just so much more fun.

Play 4 times
(last X)

What   peo - ple just don't un - der - stand is   that   writ-ing's de -

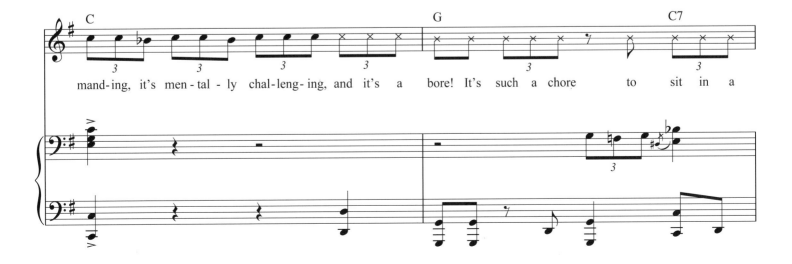

mand-ing, it's men - tal - ly chal - leng - ing, and it's a   bore! It's such a chore   to sit in a

I CAIN'T SAY NO

from OKLAHOMA!

Lyrics by OSCAR HAMMERSTEIN II
Music by RICHARD RODGERS

52

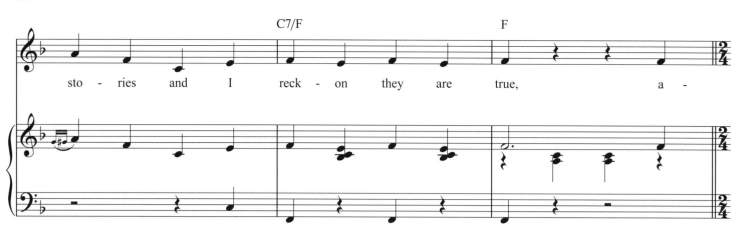

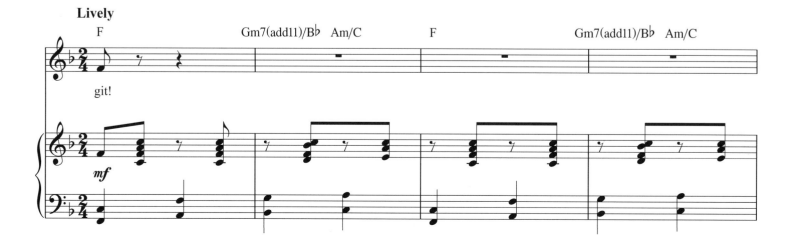

Refrain

I'm just a girl who cain't say no,
I'm just a girl who cain't say no,

I'm in a ter - ri - ble fix. _____
cain't seem to say it at all. _____

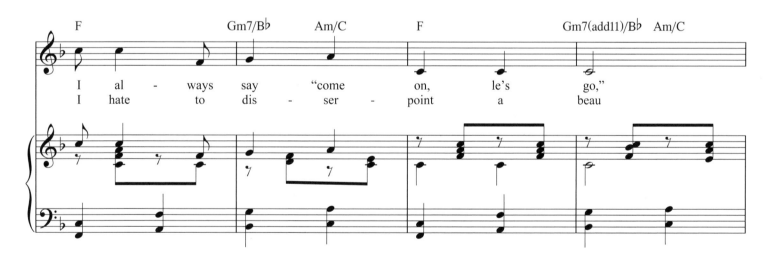

I al - ways say "come on, le's go,"
I hate to dis - ser - point a beau

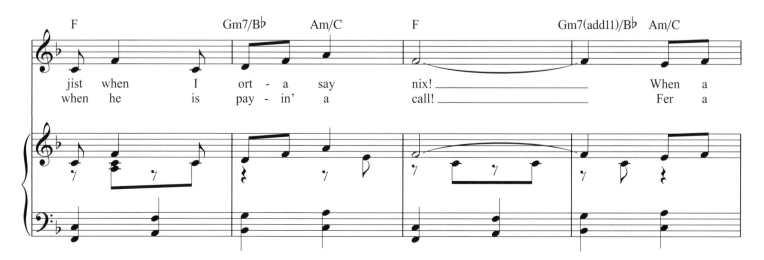

jist when I ort - a say nix! _____ When a
when he is pay - in' a call! _____ Fer a

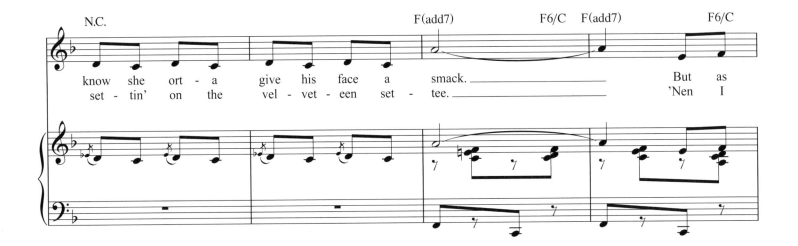

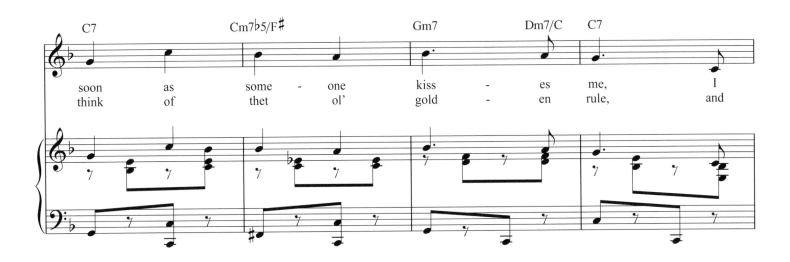

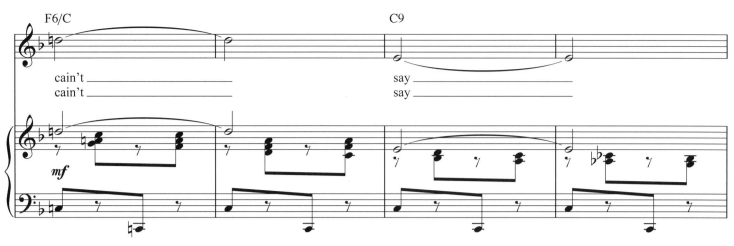

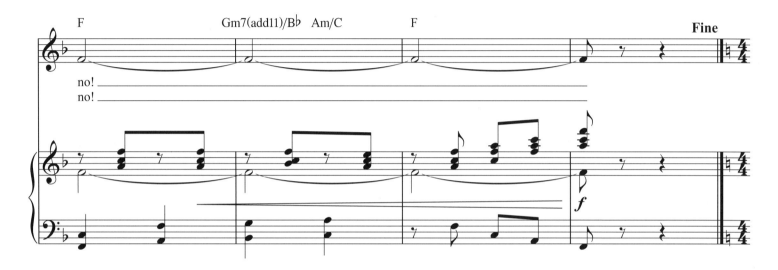

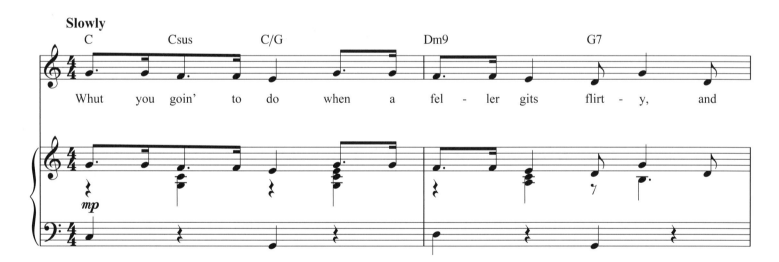

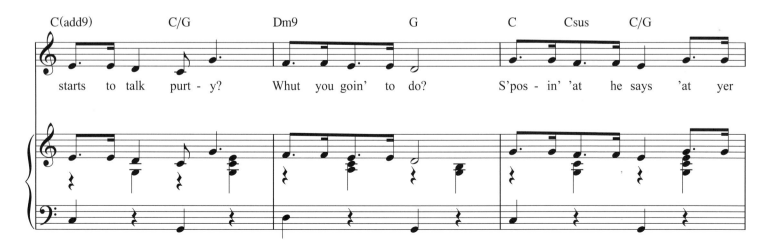

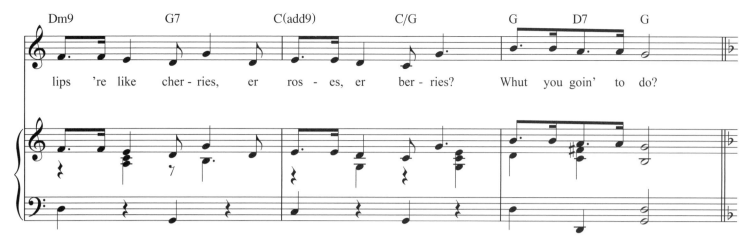

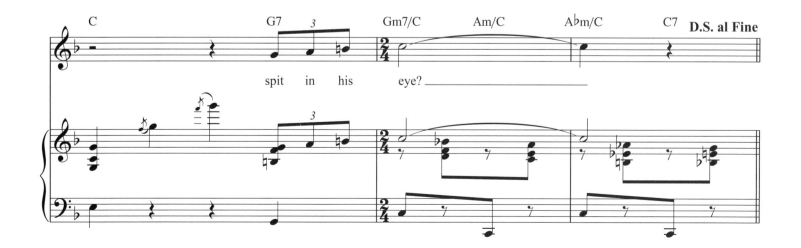

HE VAS MY BOYFRIEND
from YOUNG FRANKENSTEIN

Music and Lyrics by
MEL BROOKS

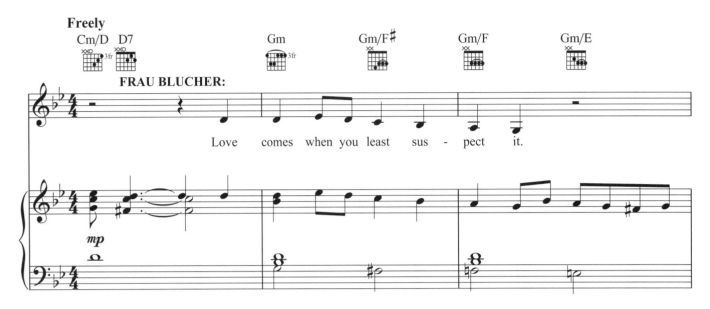

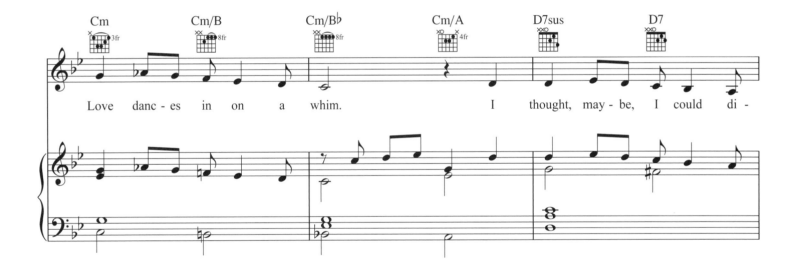

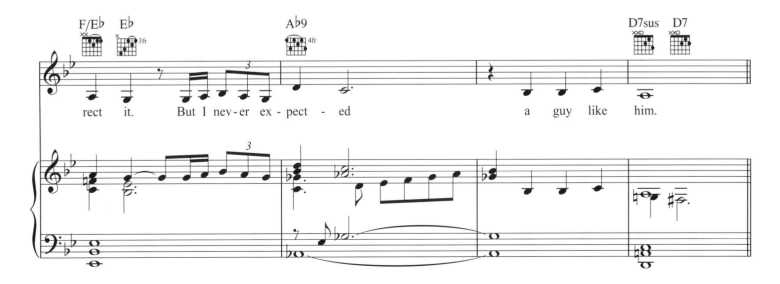

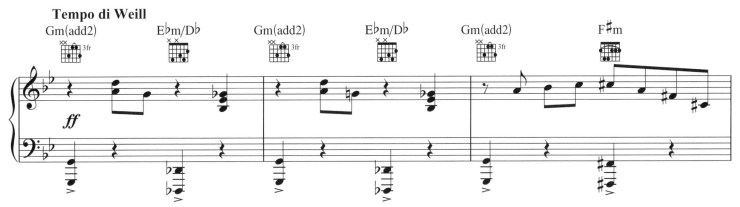

Tempo di Weill

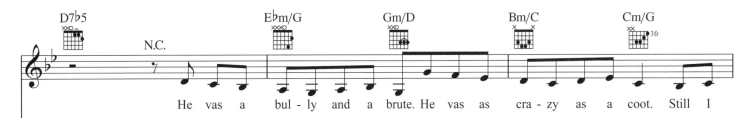

He vas a bul-ly and a brute. He vas as cra-zy as a coot. Still I

did-n't give a hoot, he vas my boy - friend.

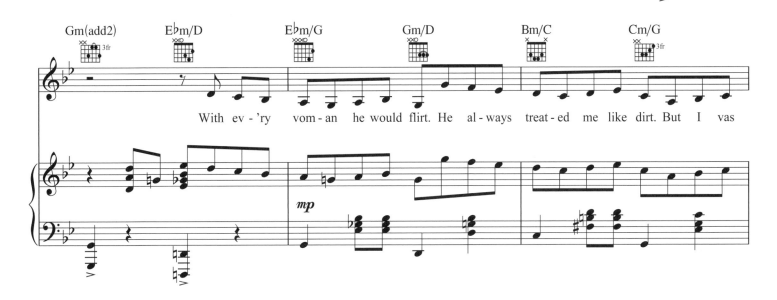

With ev-'ry vom-an he would flirt. He al-ways treat-ed me like dirt. But I vas

he vas a dirty old goat. Ve were made for each other. All of a sudden, he took out his paraphernalia and shouted, "Let's play croquet!" And off to the field ve vent. He carried his hoops and mallets and I carried his balls. What a festival! Fun and games all day long. Archery, badminton, potato sack. Victor won the three-legged race… all by himself.

It vas love at first sight.

He vas the one who I gave my heart to, but ve nev - er wed, e - ven so.

If I men - tioned wed - lock, he'd put me in a head - lock.

HEIL MYSELF
from THE PRODUCERS

Music and Lyrics by
MEL BROOKS

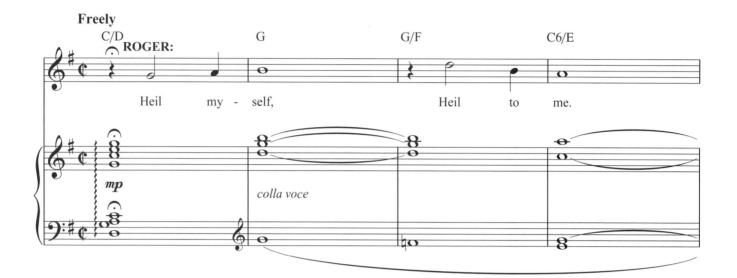

Roger is joined by ensemble in this production number, adapted as a solo here.

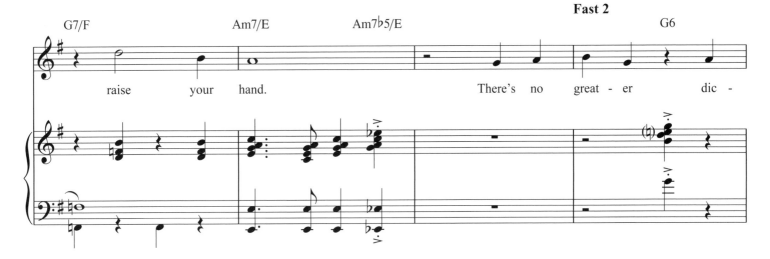

Fast 2

raise your hand. There's no great-er dic -

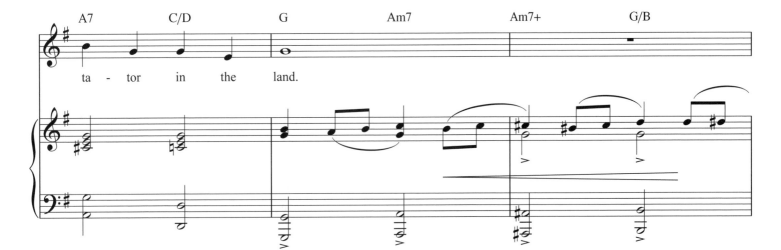

ta - tor in the land.

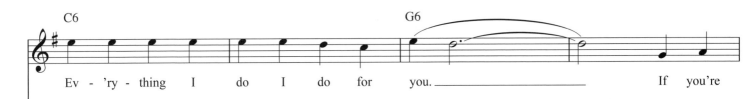

Ev - 'ry - thing I do I do for you._____ If you're

look - ing for a war, here's World War Two. Heil my -

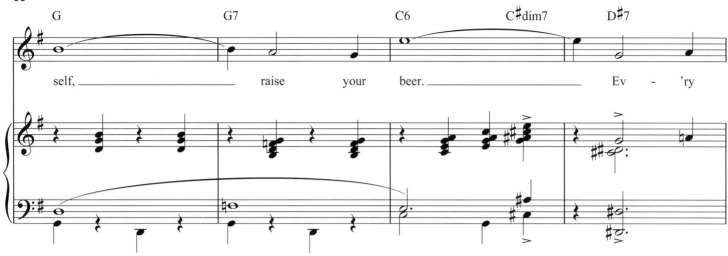

self, _____ raise your beer. _____ Ev - 'ry

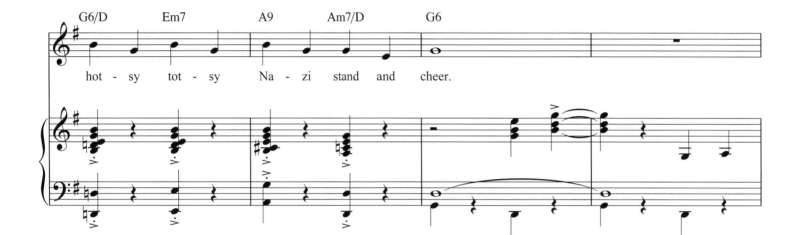

hot - sy tot - sy Na - zi stand and cheer.

Heil my - self! _____

Heil my - self! _____

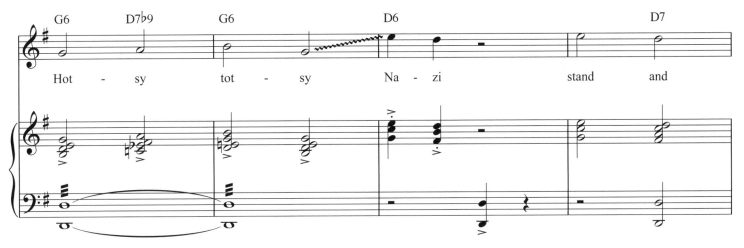

I AM ALDOLPHO
from THE DROWSY CHAPERONE

Words and Music by LISA LAMBERT
and GREG MORRISON

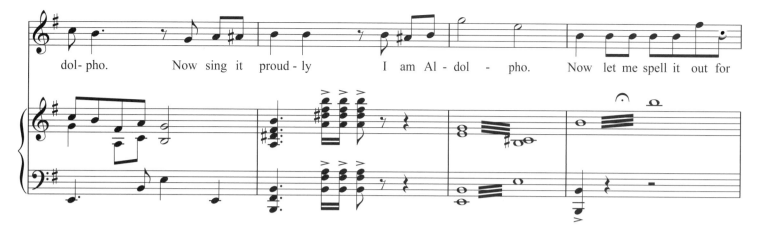

dol- pho. Now sing it proud - ly I am Al - dol - pho. Now let me spell it out for

you *for all you lovely ladies who didn't hear,*
for some reason maybe you are hard of
hearing or something – I don't know. It goes

a - a - a - a - a - al

[colla voce]

do - ho - ho - ho - ho - hol   f - f - f - f - f - fo   I am Al - dol - pho _____

_____ Al - dol - pho!

I DON'T UNDERSTAND THE POOR
from A GENTLEMAN'S GUIDE TO LOVE & MURDER

Music by STEVEN LUTVAK
Lyrics by ROBERT L. FREEDMAN
and STEVEN LUTVAK

LORD ADALBERT: *I say! You, there!*

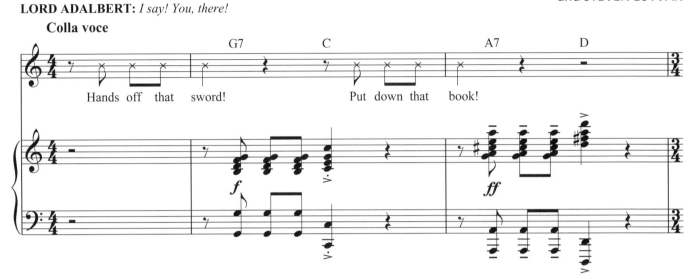

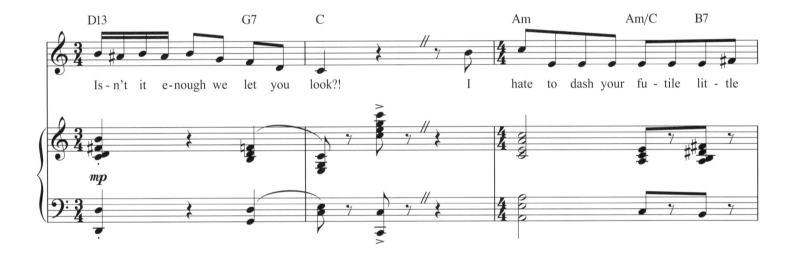

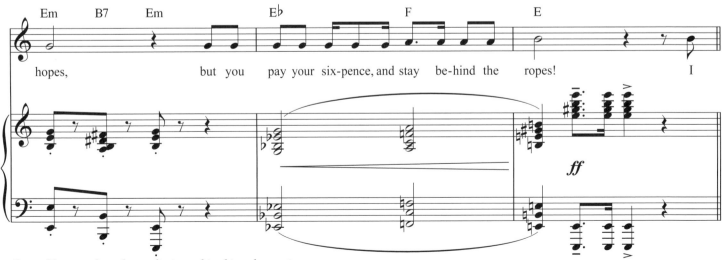

Ensemble parts have been eliminated in this solo version.

Con moto

cringe when ev - 'ry cob - bler or butch - er or farm - er comes touch - ing my ban - ni - sters,

bang - ing my ar - mour. They fin - ger ev - 'ry fin - i - al. They poke your cor - ner - stone. Who'd

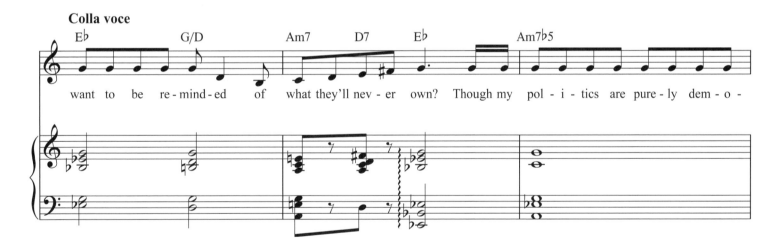

Colla voce

want to be re - mind - ed of what they'll nev - er own? Though my pol - i - tics are pure - ly dem - o -

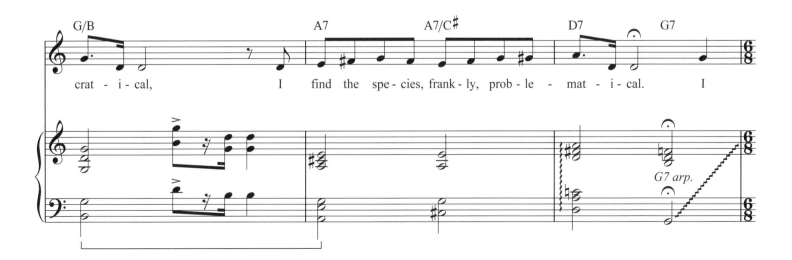

crat - i - cal, I find the spe - cies, frank - ly, prob - le - mat - i - cal. I

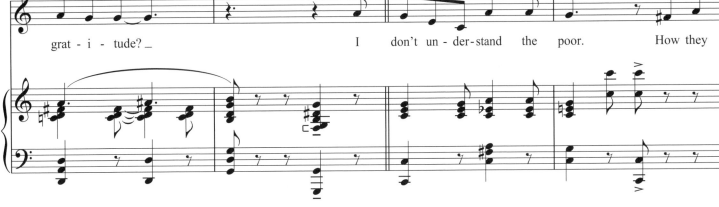

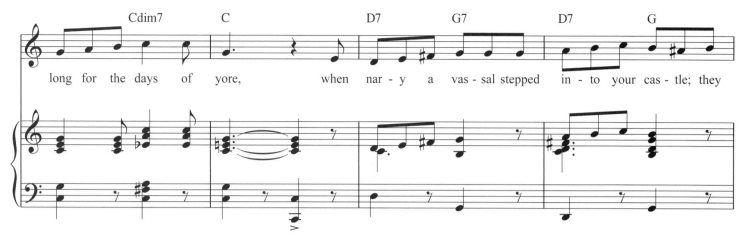

long for the days of yore, when nar-y a vas-sal stepped in-to your cas-tle; they

knew not to dark-en your door. Now they barge in ev-er-y Tues-day,___ with a

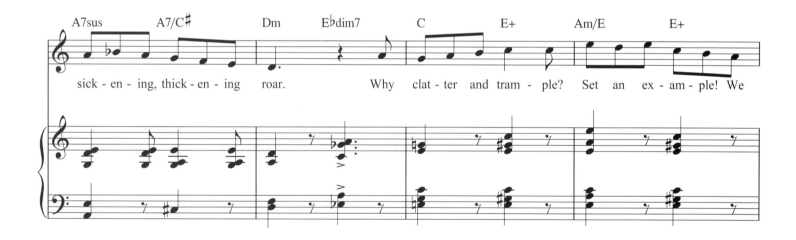

sick-en-ing, thick-en-ing roar. Why clat-ter and tram-ple? Set an ex-am-ple! We

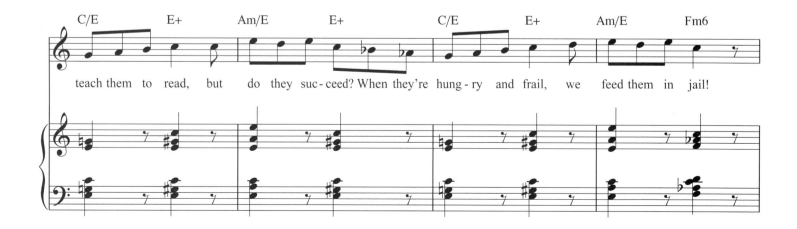

teach them to read, but do they suc-ceed? When they're hung-ry and frail, we feed them in jail!

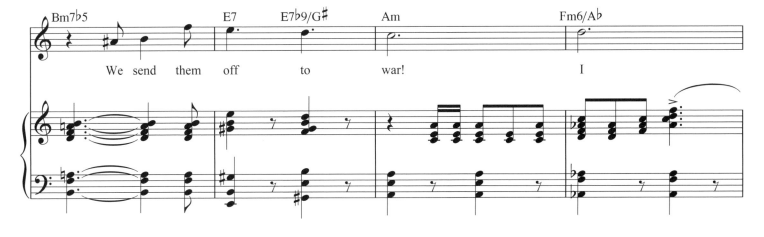

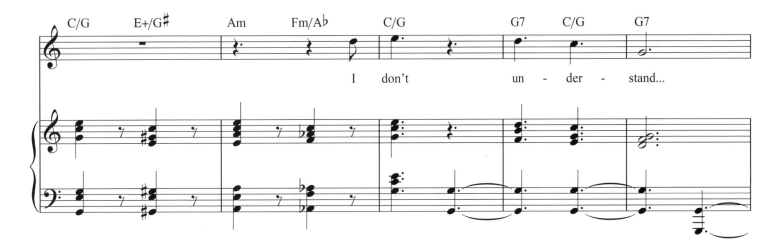

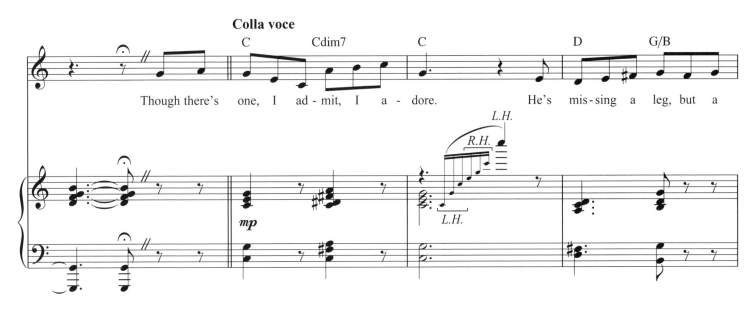

ver - y good egg, a gen - tle - man through to the core. He may be a bit of a

drink - er; he can of - ten be found on the floor. Through all of his pains, he

nev - er com - plains. He's bright and as - tute, a shame that he's mute. Ac - cord - ing to Moth - er, he

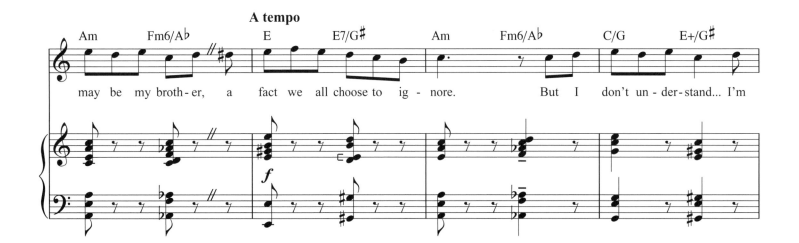

may be my broth - er, a fact we all choose to ig - nore. But I don't un - der - stand... I'm

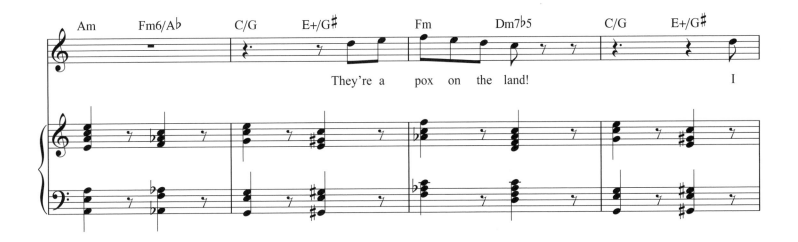

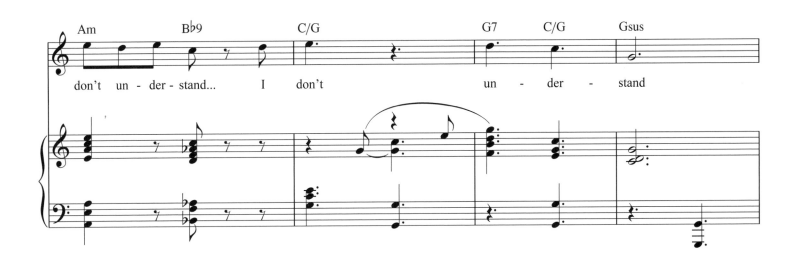

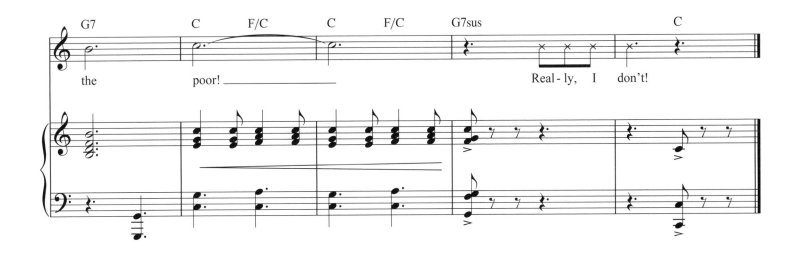

I'M NOT WEARING UNDERWEAR TODAY

from the Broadway Musical AVENUE Q

Music and Lyrics by ROBERT LOPEZ
and JEFF MARX

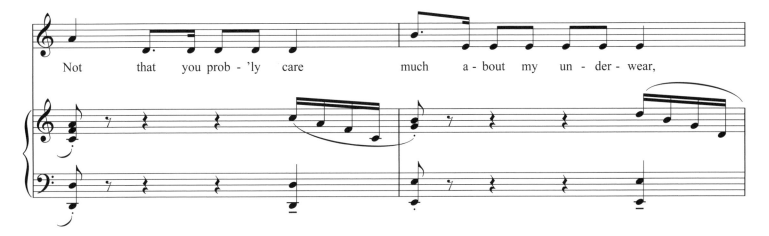

Not that you prob - 'ly care much a - bout my un - der - wear,

still, none - the - less I got - ta say, _____

___ that I'm not wear - ing

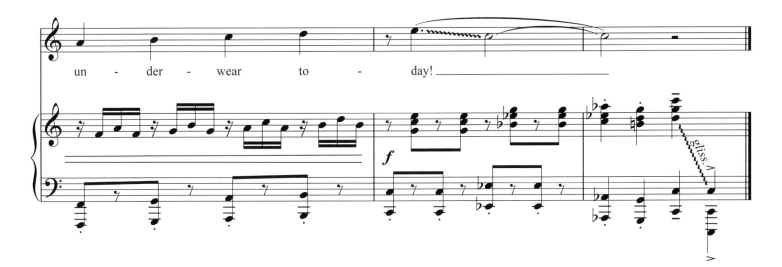

un - der - wear to - day! _____

IF YOU WERE GAY

from the Broadway Musical AVENUE Q

Music and Lyrics by ROBERT LOPEZ
and JEFF MARX

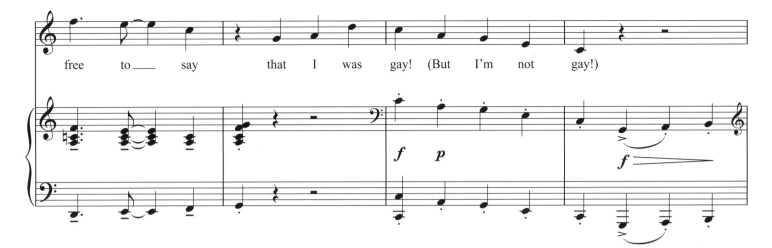

free to ___ say that I was gay! (But I'm not gay!)

If you were

queer, I'd still be here, year af - ter

year, be - cause you're dear to ___ me. And I know that

If you were gay, I'd shout hoo-ray! And here I'd stay, But I would-n't get in your ___ way. You can count on me to al-ways

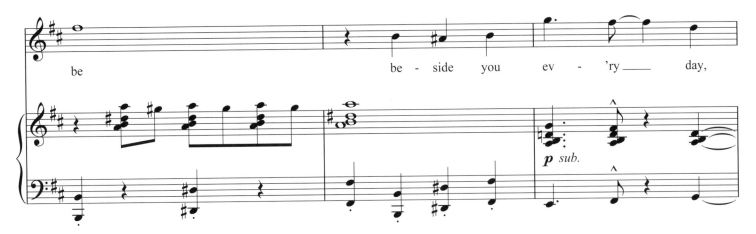

be

be - side you ev - 'ry ___ day,

to tell you it's o - kay,   You were just born that ___ way,

And as they say: It's in your D - N - A,   you're

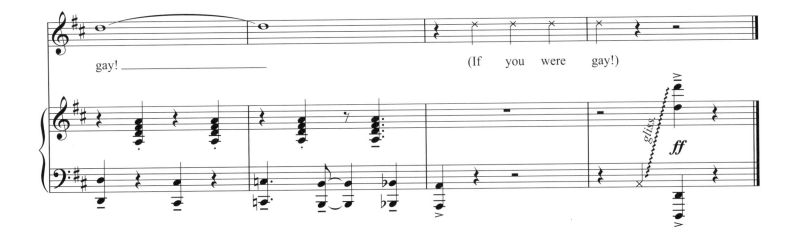

gay! _____   (If you were gay!)

KIDS!
from BYE BYE BIRDIE

Lyric by LEE ADAMS
Music by CHARLES STROUSE

dis - o - be - di - ent, dis - re - spect - ful oafs! ____
so ri - dic - u - lous and so im - ma - ture! ____

Nois - y cra - zy slop - py la - zy loaf - ers! ____
I don't see why an - y - bod - y wants 'em! ____

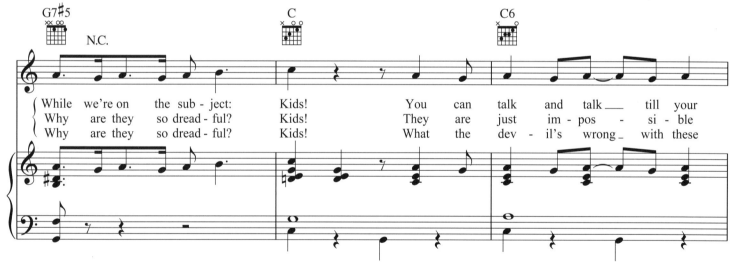

While we're on the sub - ject: Kids! You can talk and talk ____ till your
Why are they so dread - ful? Kids! They are just im - pos - si - ble
Why are they so dread - ful? Kids! What the dev - il's wrong ____ with these

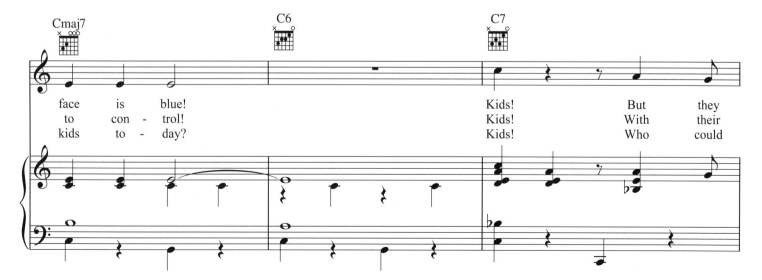

face is blue! Kids! But they
to con - trol! Kids! With their
kids to - day? Kids! Who could

LES POISSONS

from THE LITTLE MERMAID – A Broadway Musical

Music by ALAN MENKEN
Lyrics by HOWARD ASHMAN

Bright Waltz

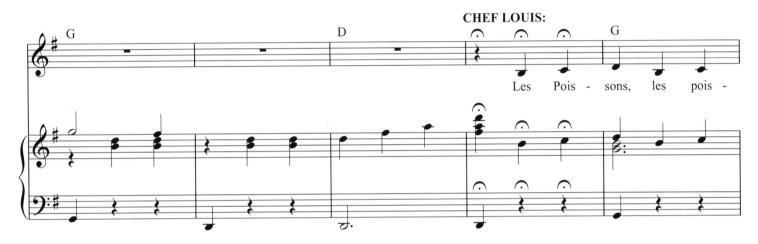

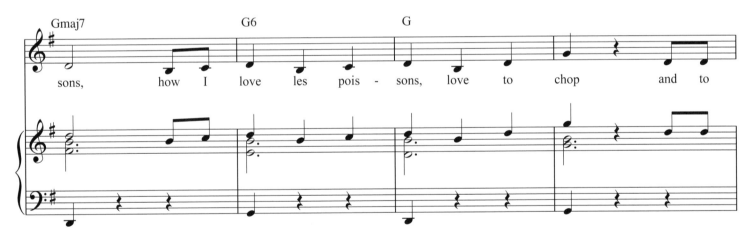

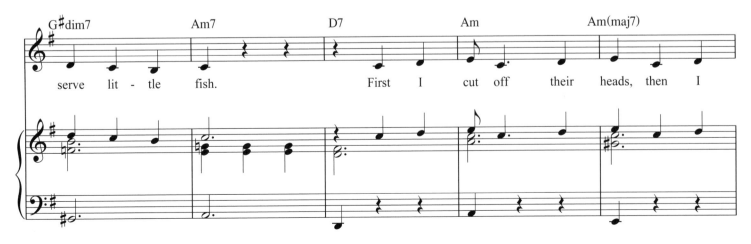

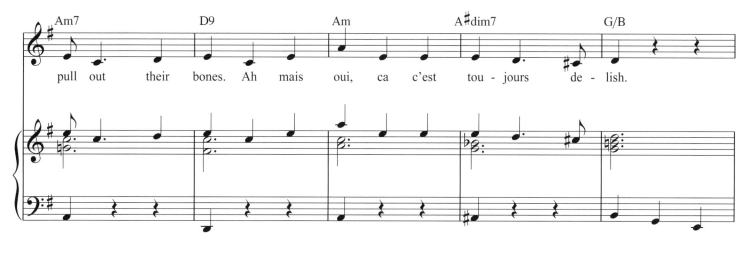

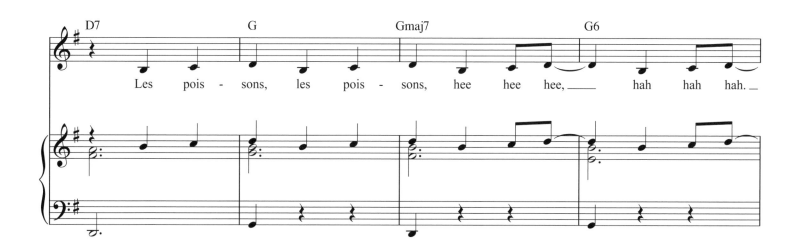

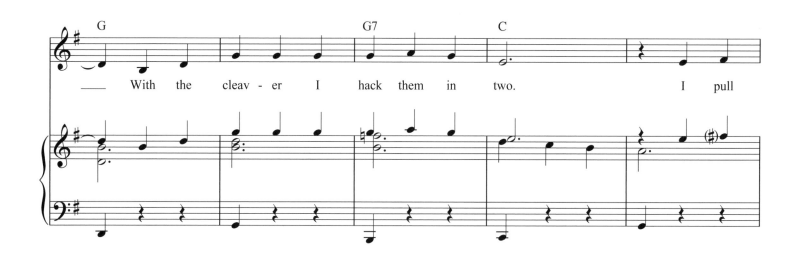

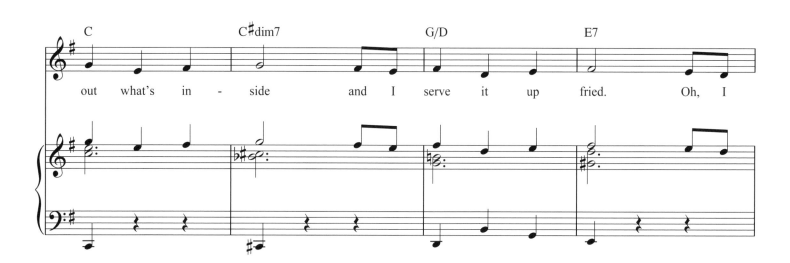

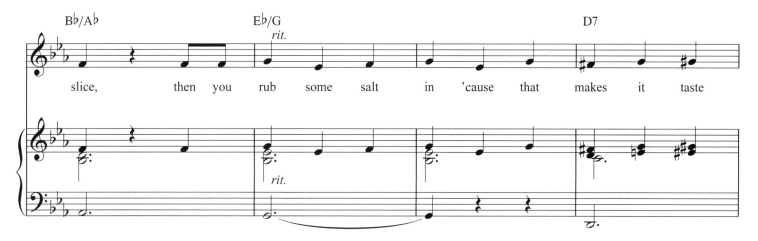

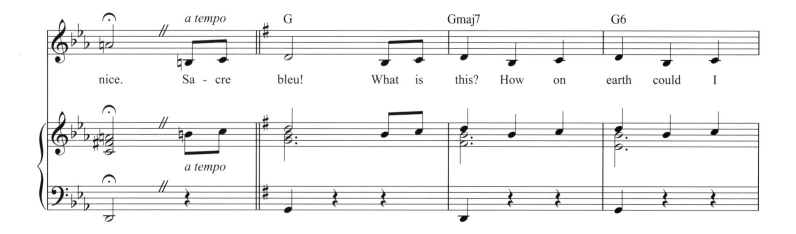

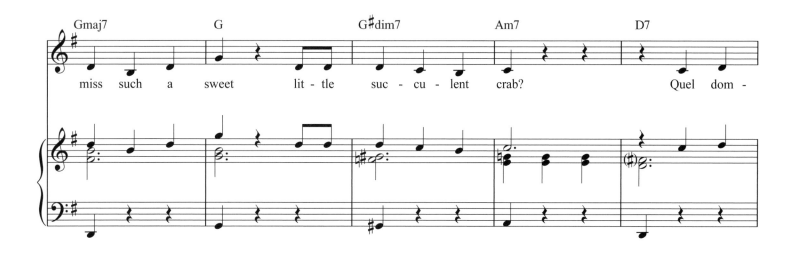

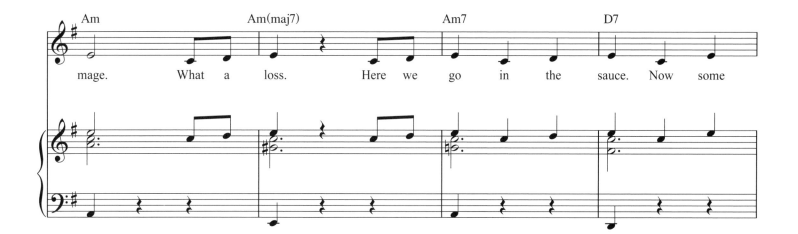

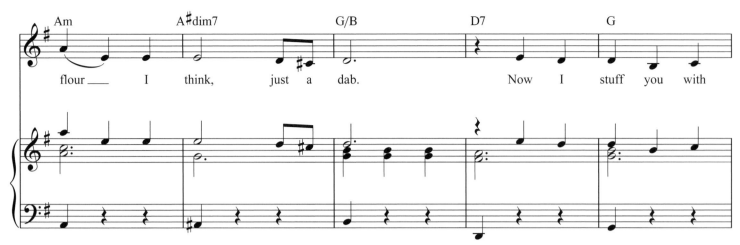

flour ___ I think, just a dab. Now I stuff you with

bread. It don't hurt 'cause you're dead. And you're cer - tain - ly luck - y you

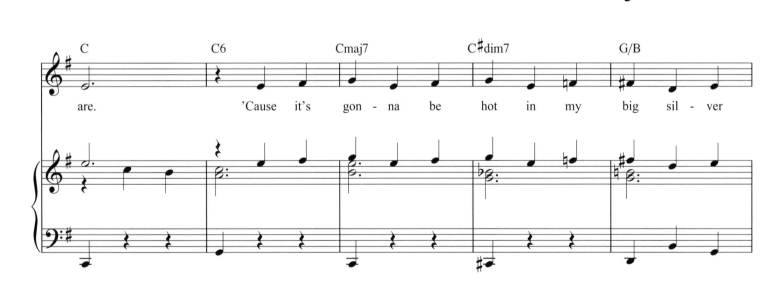

are. 'Cause it's gon - na be hot in my big sil - ver

pot. Too - dle loo, mon pois - son, au re - voir!

LOVE IS MY LEGS

from DIRTY ROTTEN SCOUNDRELS

Words and Music by
DAVID YAZBEK

Moderate Rock Ballad

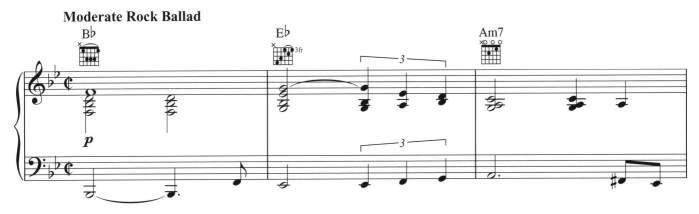

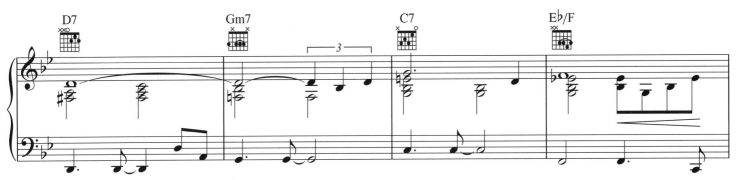

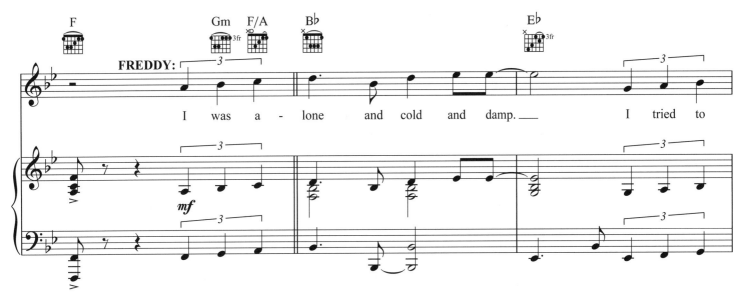

FREDDY:

I was a - lone and cold and damp. ___ I tried to

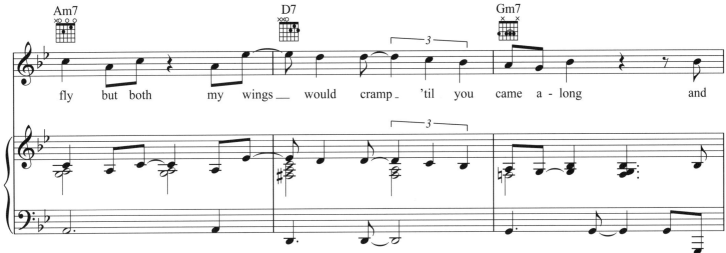

fly but both my wings ___ would cramp ___ 'til you came a - long and

1. **F:** *Oh, my God! I did it. I'm walking!*   **C:** *Do you want to rest?*   **F:** *No, I want to keep going. My legs are*
2. **C:** *Here?*   **F:** *Further*   **C:** *How far do you want to go?*

full of love. Stand over there.   **F:** *All the way!*

CHRISTINE:
The leg-bone's con - nect - ed to an - kle bones, con - nect - ed to feet-bones of

FREDDY:
Love is my legs and you are my love, so you are my feet-bones of

ME

from BEAUTY AND THE BEAST: THE BROADWAY MUSICAL

Music by ALAN MENKEN
Lyrics by TIM RICE

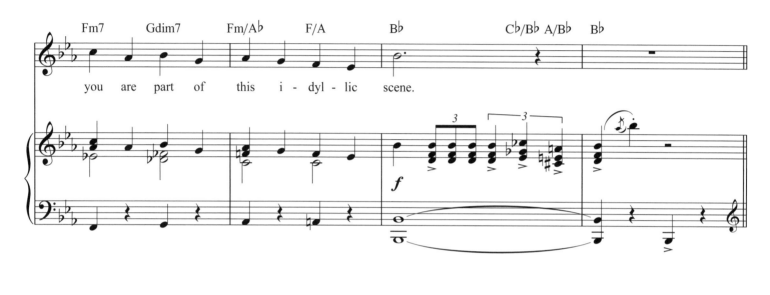

keep - ing house with pride. Each day, grat - i - fied

you are part of this i - dyl - lic scene.

(Spoken:) Picture this: A rustic hunting lodge... my latest kill, roasting over the fire... my little wife massaging my feet...

while the little ones play on the floor with the dogs. Oh, we'll have six or seven!

lead to... The best things in life are... All's well that ends with

me! _____ Es - cape me? There's no way. Cer - tain as

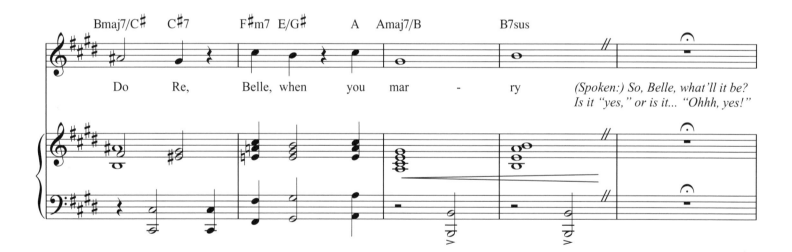

Do Re, Belle, when you mar - ry *(Spoken:) So, Belle, what'll it be?*
Is it "yes," or is it... "Ohhh, yes!"

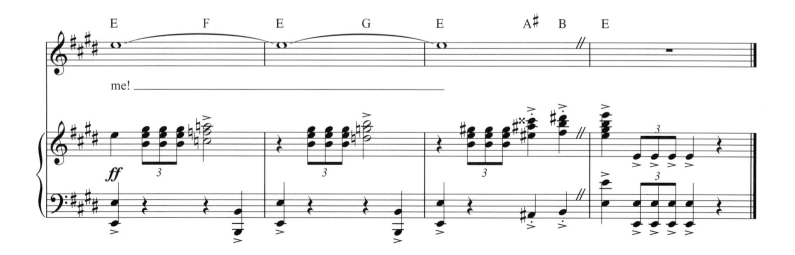

me! _____

REAL LIVE GIRL
from LITTLE ME

Music by CY COLEMAN
Lyrics by CAROLYN LEIGH

Fred is joined by an ensemble of soldiers, adapted here as a solo edition.

real _____ live _____ girl. _____

a tempo

Noth - ing can beat get - ting swept off your

feet by a real live girl.

Dreams in your bunk don't com - pare with a hunk of a real

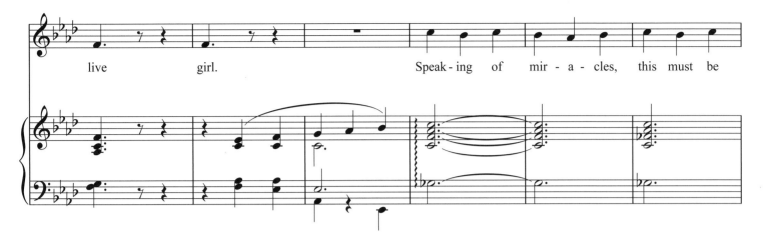

live girl. Speak - ing of mir - a - cles, this must be

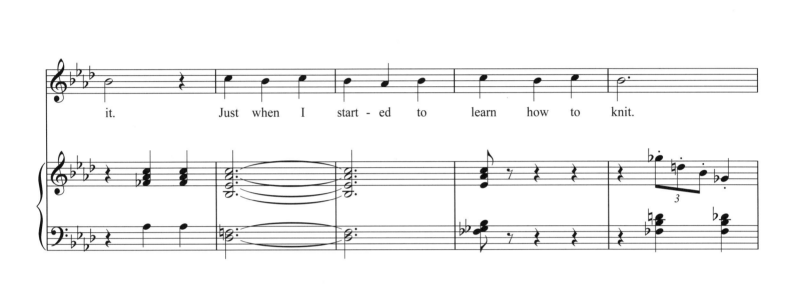

it. Just when I start - ed to learn how to knit.

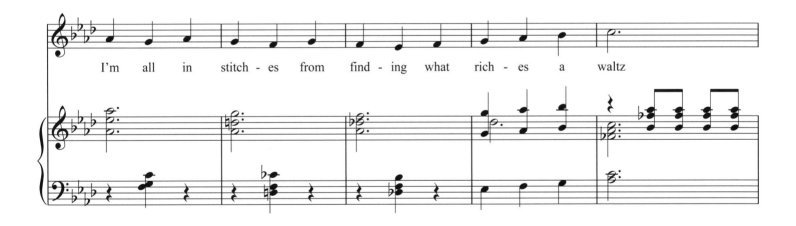

I'm all in stitch - es from find - ing what rich - es a waltz

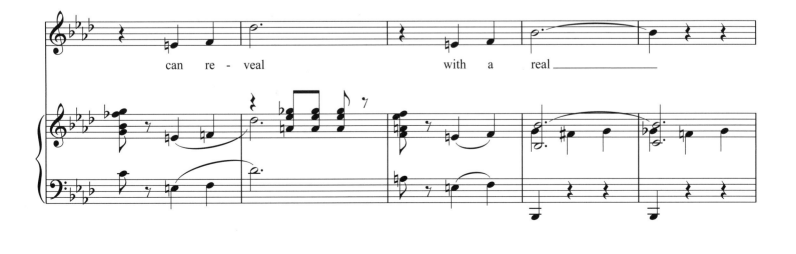

can re - veal with a real _____

live _____ girl.

I've seen pho - to - graphs and fac - sim - i - les that have

set my heart off in a whirl, but

no work of art gets you right in the heart like a real

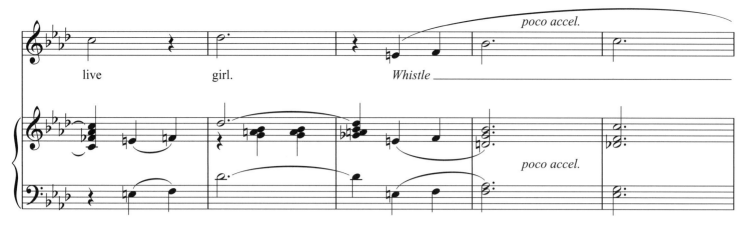

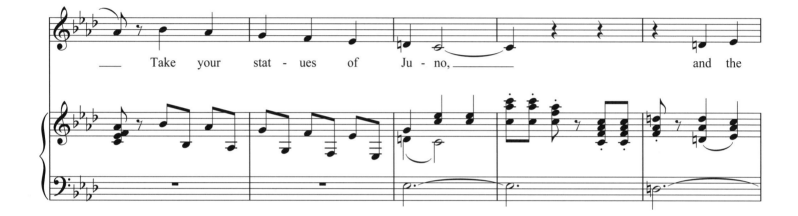

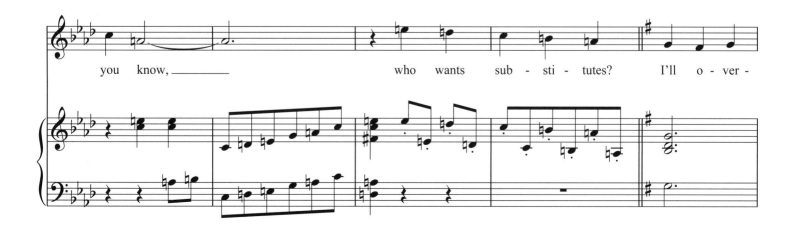

look ev - 'ry one in the book for a real sex - y Sal - ly or Lu - la - belle. _____

_____ Take your Ve - ne - tian or Ro - man or Gre - cian i - deal, I'll take

some - thing more use - a - ble. Girls were like fel - las was once my be -

lief, what a re - ver - sal and what a re - lief.

118

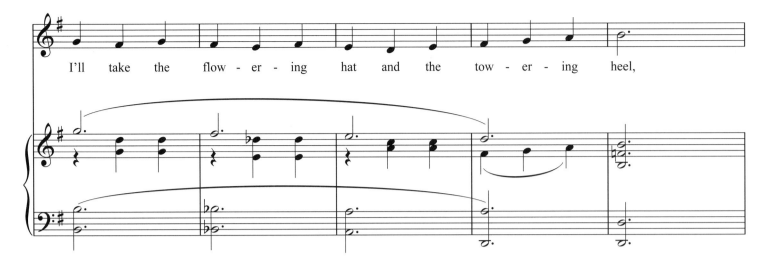

I'll take the flow - er - ing hat and the tow - er - ing heel,

and the squeal of a real

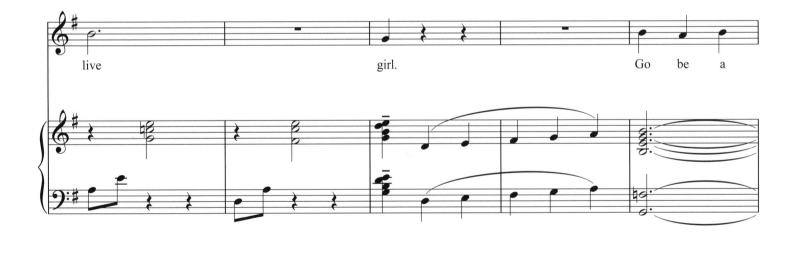

live girl. Go be a

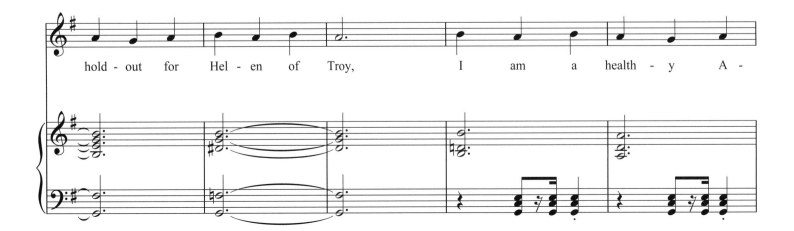

hold - out for Hel - en of Troy, I am a health - y A -

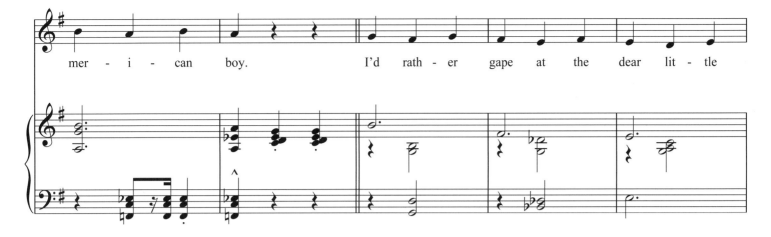

mer - i - can boy. I'd rath - er gape at the dear lit - tle

shape and the stern, and the keel of a

Broadly, in 3   **A tempo**

full - time vo - ca - tion - al all op - er - a - tion - al girl.

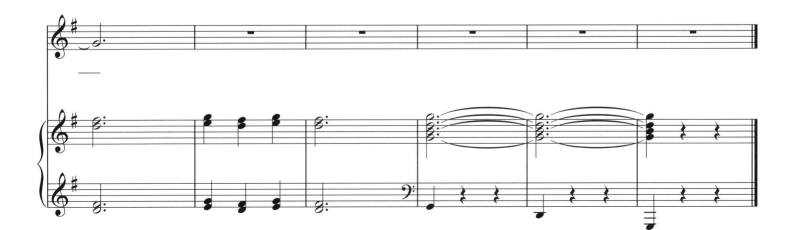

MY NEW PHILOSOPHY

from YOU'RE A GOOD MAN, CHARLIE BROWN

Music and Lyrics by
ANDREW LIPPA

SALLY: *Spoken (before the vamp): "Why are you telling me?" (beat) I like it.*

* Original key: A Major.

The song is a duet for Sally and Schroeder. The composer created this solo edition for publication.

Sal - ly Brown, _ your grades are go - ing down." _ I could have

told her my new phi - los - o - phy. (as teacher) Miss B?

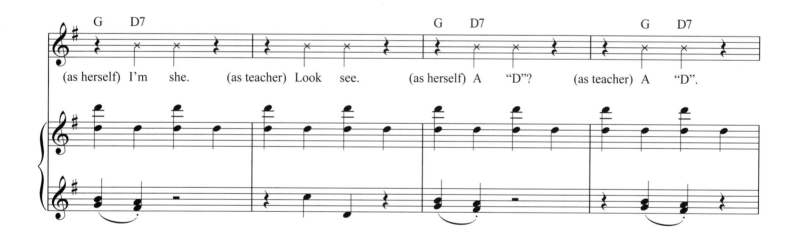

(as herself) I'm she. (as teacher) Look see. (as herself) A "D"? (as teacher) A "D".

Spoken (as herself): Well, why are you telling me? And that's my new phi - los - o - phy!! _

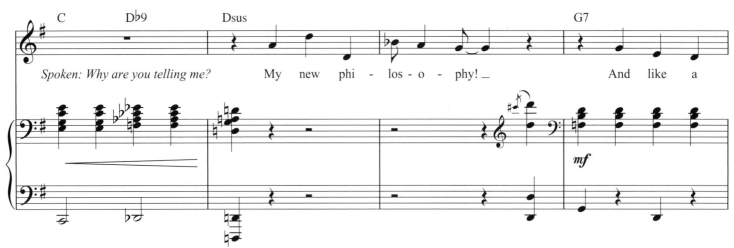

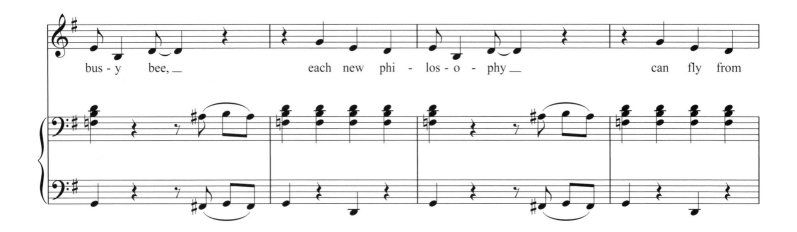

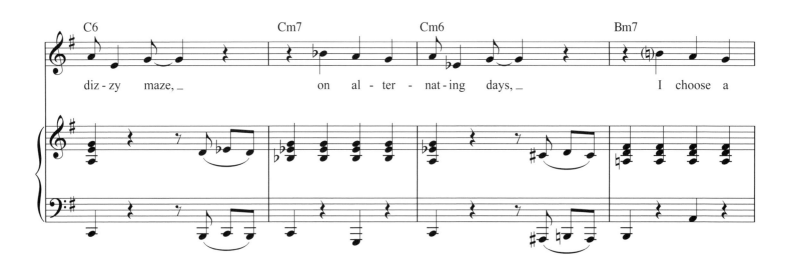

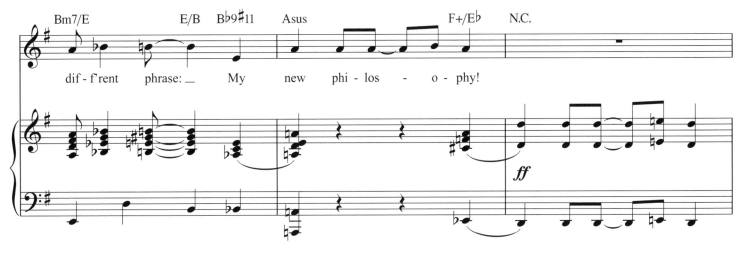

dif - f'rent phrase: _ My new phi - los - o - phy!

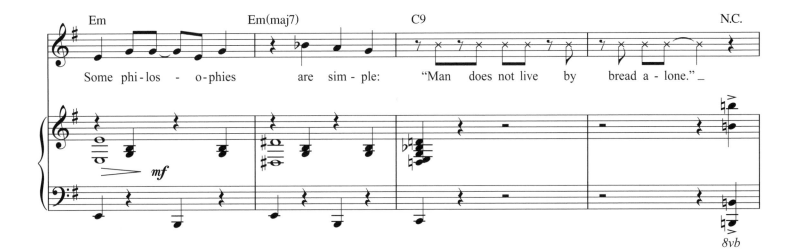

Some phi - los - o - phies are sim - ple: "Man does not live by bread a - lone." _

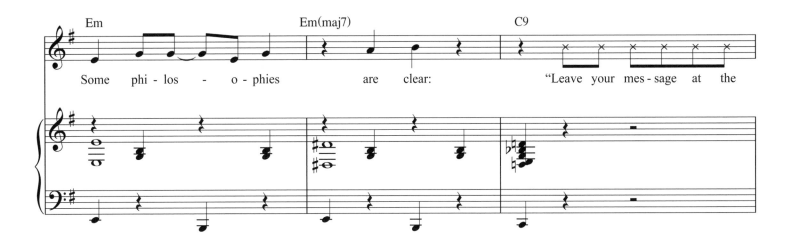

Some phi - los - o - phies are clear: "Leave your mes - sage at the

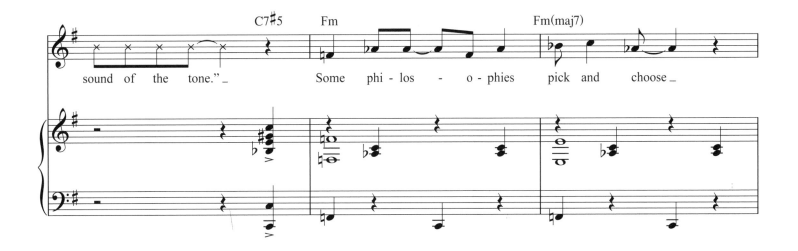

sound of the tone." _ Some phi - los - o - phies pick and choose _

NOTHING
from A CHORUS LINE

Music by MARVIN HAMLISCH
Lyric by EDWARD KLEBAN

DIANA: *I'm so excited because I'm gonna go to the High School of Performing Arts. I mean, I was dying to be a serious actress. Anyway, it's the first day of acting class and we're in the auditorium and the teacher, Mister Karp, puts us up on the stage with our legs around everybody, one in back of the other, and he says: O.K., we're going to do improvisations. Now, you're on a bobsled and it's snowing out and it's cold. O.K., go!*

127

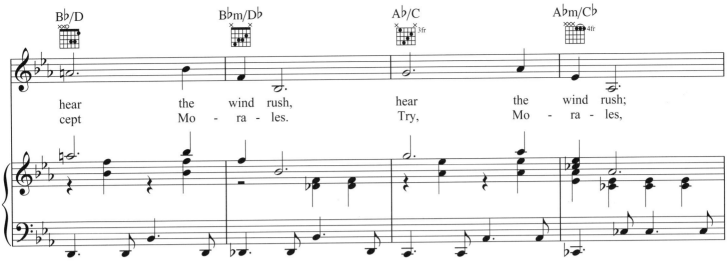

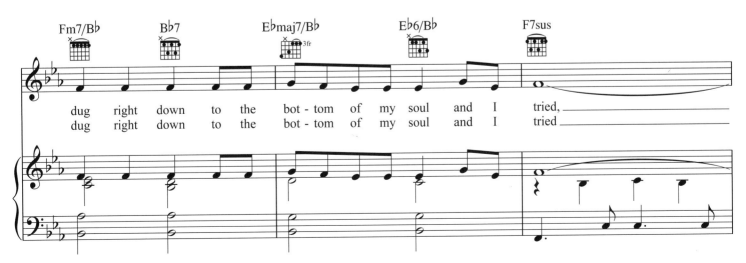

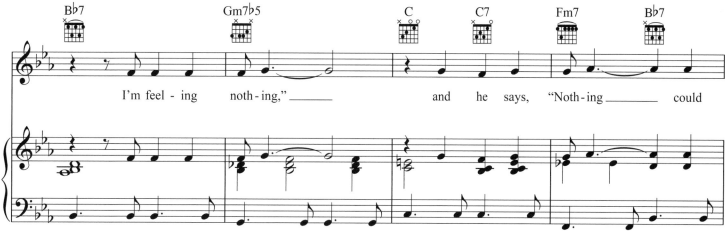

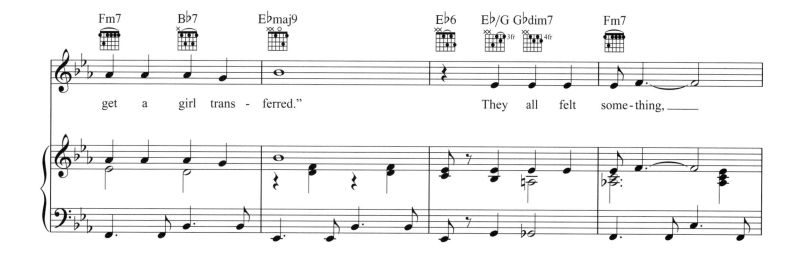

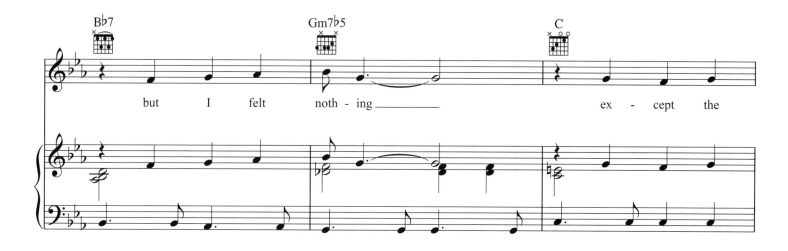

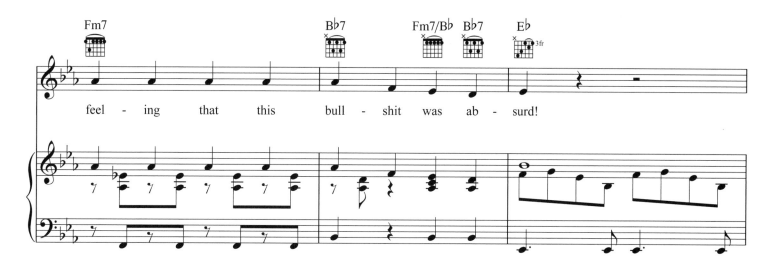

They were so help - ful. They called me "Hope - less,"

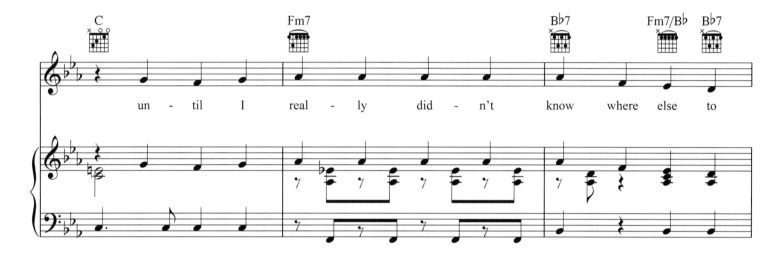

un - til I real - ly did - n't know where else to

turn. *And Karp kept saying,* *"Morales, I think you should transfer to Girls' High.*

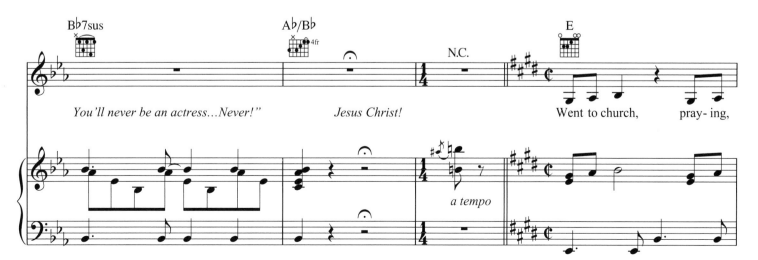

You'll never be an actress…Never!" *Jesus Christ!* Went to church, pray- ing,

a tempo

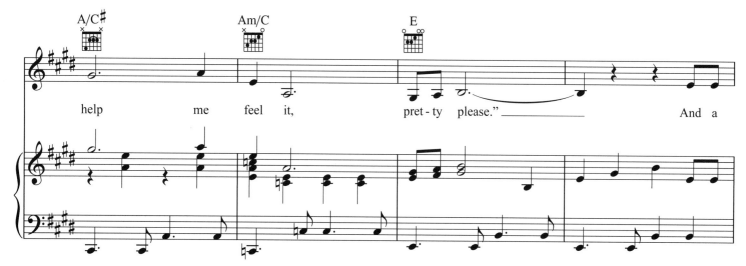

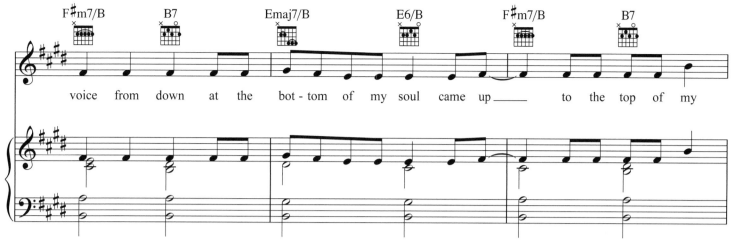

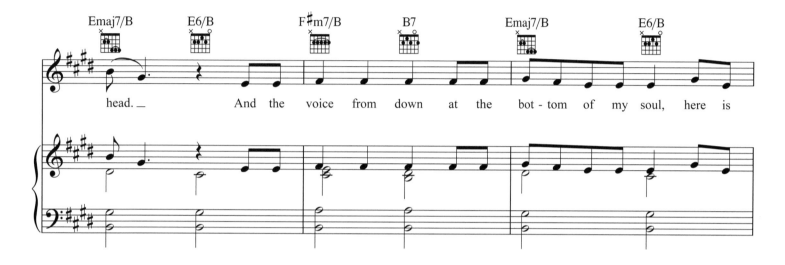

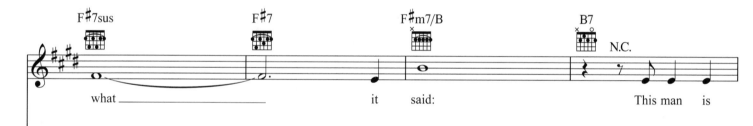

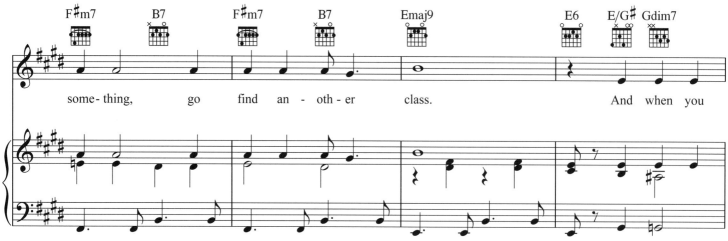

some- thing, go find an - oth - er class. And when you

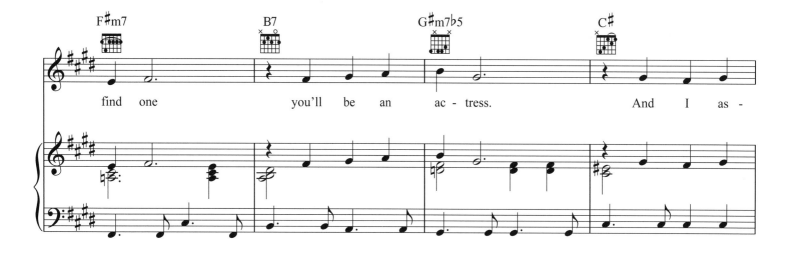

find one you'll be an ac - tress. And I as -

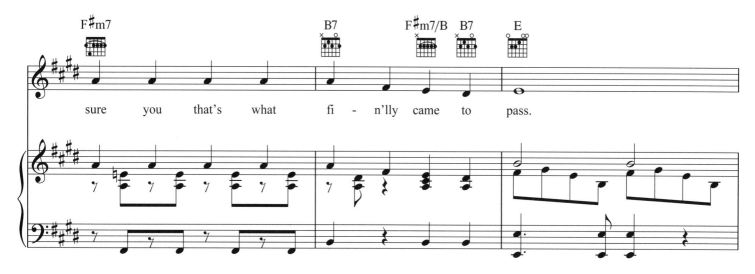

sure you that's what fi - n'lly came to pass.

Slower, ad lib.

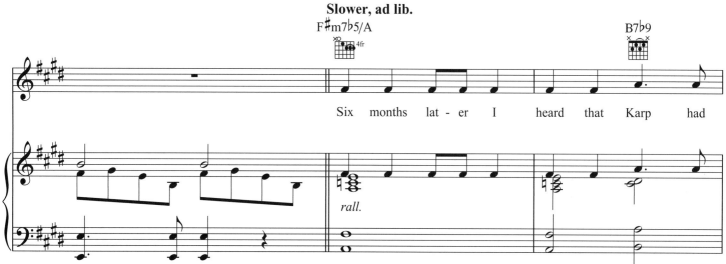

Six months lat - er I heard that Karp had

ONE HUNDRED EASY WAYS
TO LOSE A MAN

from WONDERFUL TOWN

Lyrics by BETTY COMDEN
and ADOLPH GREEN
Music by LEONARD BERNSTEIN

(Spoken flatly)
Just leap out, crawl under
the car, say it's the gasket,
and fix it in two seconds
flat with a bobby pin.

bat your eyes and say, "What __ a ro - man - tic spot we're in." __

rall.

That's a good way to lose __ a man. __ He takes you to a base - ball game, you

f a tempo   *fz*   *p*

sit knee to knee. __ He says, "The next man up at bat will bunt, you'll see." __ Don't

Just say, "Bunt? Are you nuts?!
With no outs, two men on base, and
a left-handed batter coming up, he'll
walk right into a triple play, just
like it happened in the fifth game
of the World Series in 1923."

say, "Oo, what's a bunt? This game's too hard for lit - tle me." __

rall.

life - guard at the beach that all the girl - ies a - dore___ Swims

brave-ly out to save you through the o-cean's roar. _ Don't say, "Oh, thanks, I would have drowned in

rall.

*Just push his head under
water and yell, "Last one
in is a rotten egg" and
race him back to shore.*

just one sec-ond more." _ That's a swell way to lose_ a man. _ You've

f a tempo

fz

p

found your per - fect mate and it's been love from the start.___ He

140

8/29/2017 10:48:32 AM J:\Open_Jobs\8\1211448\Music\623450\623450#.sib kbrand

OUT OF THE SUN

from HONEYMOON IN VEGAS

Music and Lyrics by
JASON ROBERT BROWN

SHOW OFF
from THE DROWSY CHAPERONE

Words and Music by Lisa Lambert
and Greg Morrison

Janet is joined by chorus in this number, edited here as a solo.

this no more _ play the sauc - y Swiss miss no more _

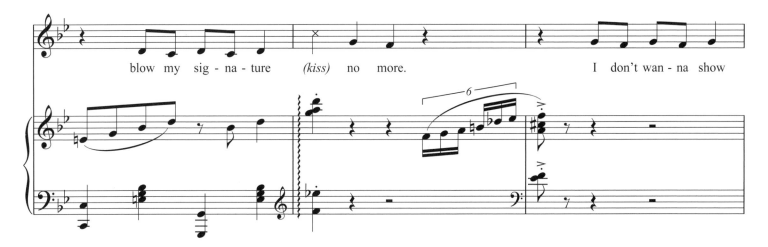

blow my sig - na - ture *(kiss)* no more. I don't wan - na show

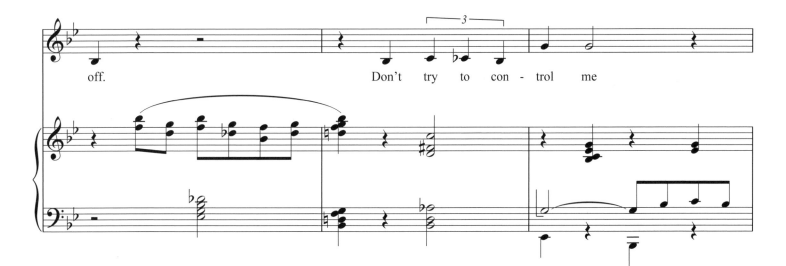

off. Don't try to con - trol me

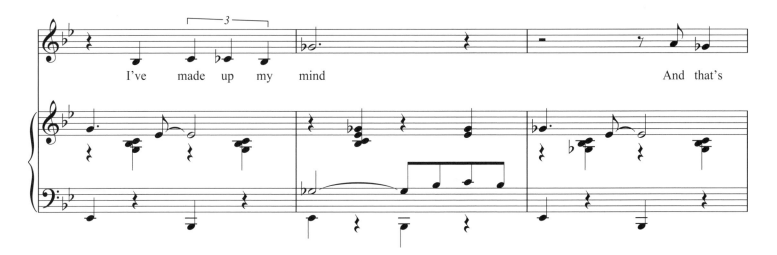

I've made up my mind And that's

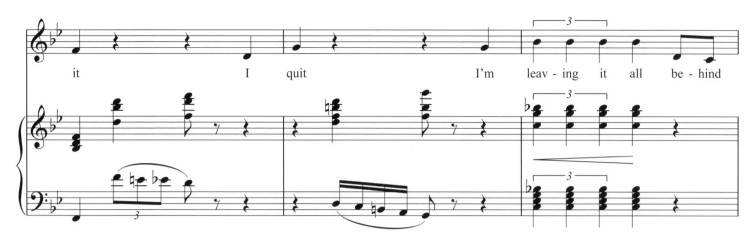

it   I   quit   I'm   leav - ing   it   all   be - hind

I   don't wan - na be

cute   no   more   Make the gen - tle - men   hoot   no   more.

I   don't wan - na wear   fruit   no   more.   I   don't wan - na show

off.

I don't wan-na show off no more _ Not

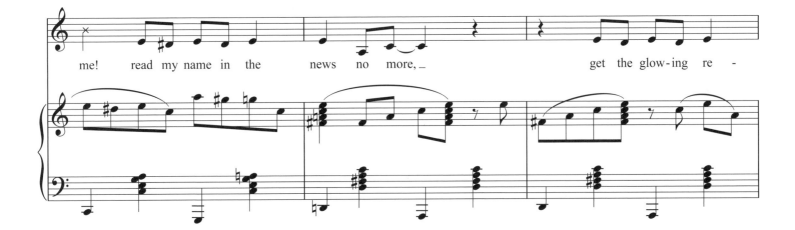

me! read my name in the news no more, _ get the glow-ing re -

views no more, Ah gee! I don't wan-na show off!

I don't want to show off!

Wheee! Please no more at - ten - tion

I've count - ed to ten and I'm

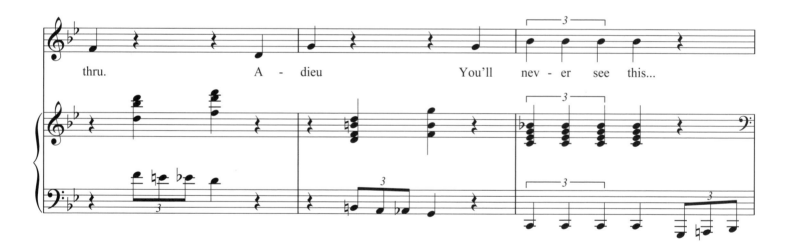

thru. A - dieu You'll nev - er see this...

(she dances)

You'll

(she dances again)

nev - er see this...

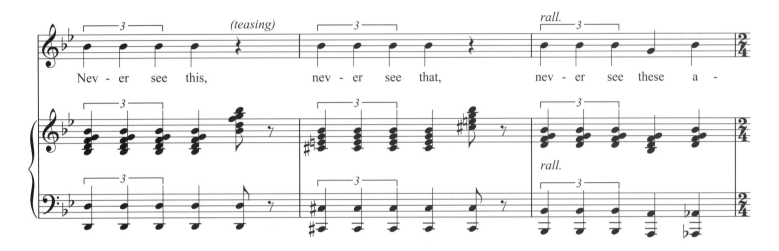

(teasing)

Never see this, nev - er see that, nev - er see these a -

rall.

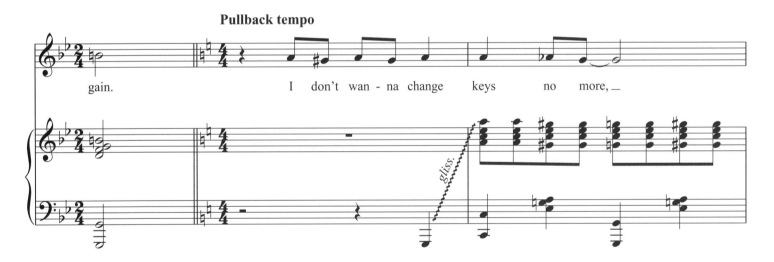

Pullback tempo

gain. I don't wan - na change keys no more, ___

gliss.

accel.

I don't wan - na strip - tease no more. I don't wan - na say

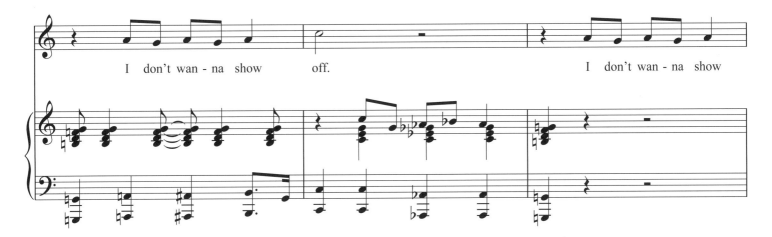

I don't wan - na show off. I don't wan - na show

Faster

off!

no more!

SHY

from ONCE UPON A MATTRESS

Words by MARSHALL BARER
Music by MARY RODGERS

Moderately, in 2

WINNIFRED:

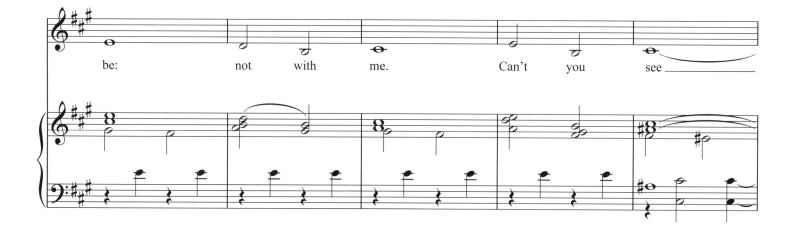

that I am just as em - bar - rassed as

poco rit.

you, and I can un - der - stand your point of view? I've al - ways been

ten.

Moderately fast, in 4

shy, I con - fess it, I'm shy. Can't you guess that this

con - fi - dent air is a mask that I wear 'cause I'm shy?

p

mf

And you may be sure, _____ way down deep, I'm de-

mure. _____ Though some peo-ple I know might de-ny it, at

bot-tom I'm qui-et and pure! _____ I'm a-ware that it's

wrong _____ to be meek as I am; my chanc-es may pass me by. I pre-tend to be

Moderately, in 2

shy. _____ Though a

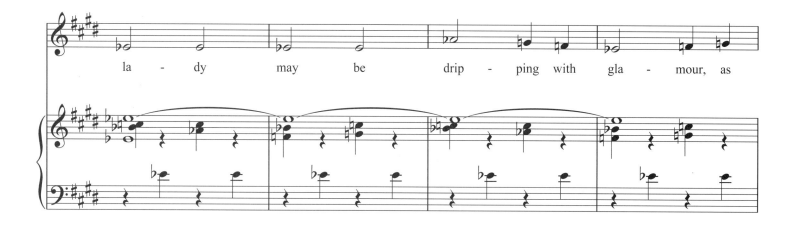

la - dy may be drip - ping with gla - mour, as

oft - en as not, she - 'll stum - ble and stam - mer when

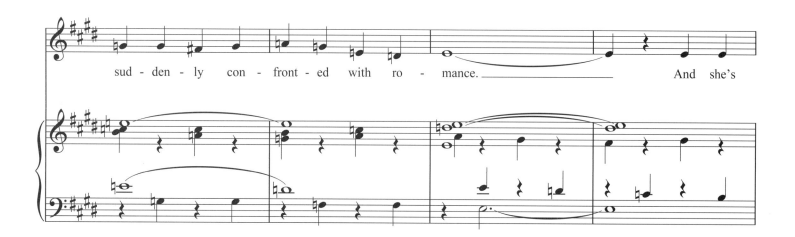

sud - den - ly con - front - ed with ro - mance. _____ And she's

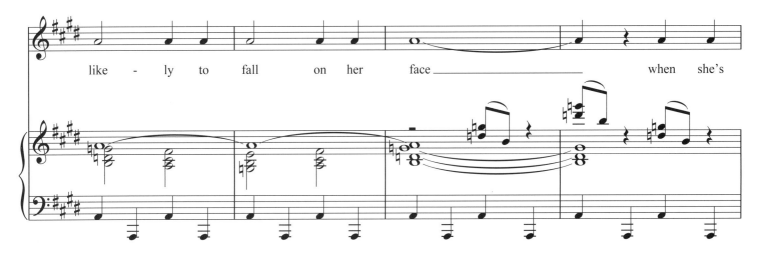

like - ly to fall on her face _____ when she's

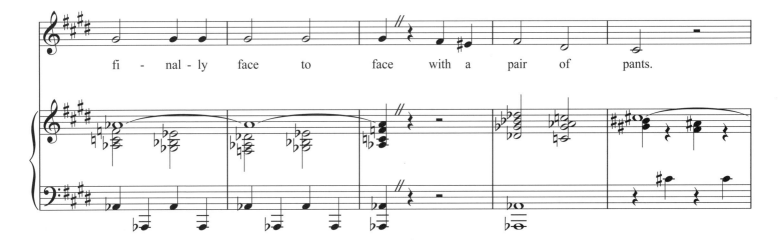

fi - nal - ly face to face with a pair of pants.

Quite oft - en, the la - dy's not as

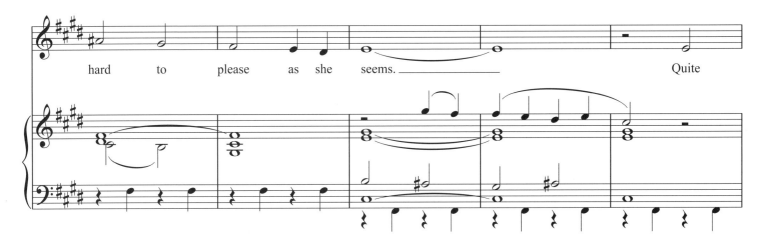

hard to please as she seems. _____ Quite

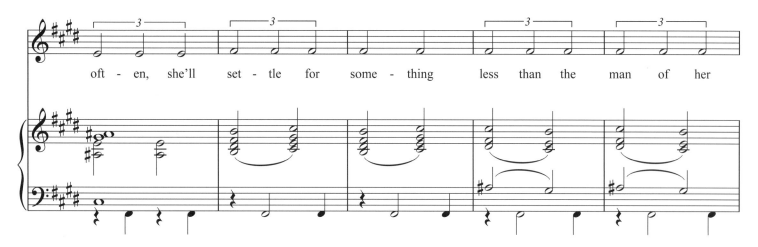

oft - en, she'll set - tle for some - thing less than the man of her

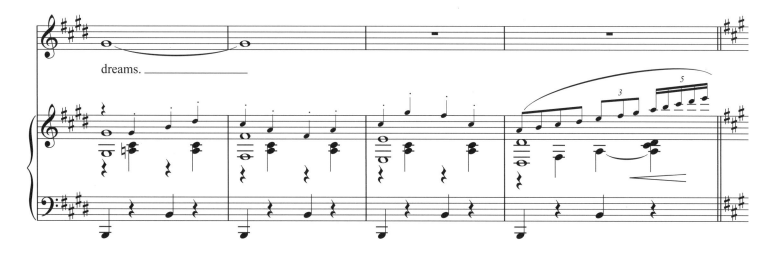

dreams. _____

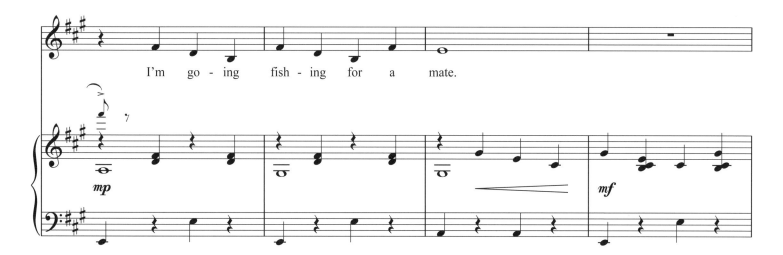

I'm go - ing fish - ing for a mate.

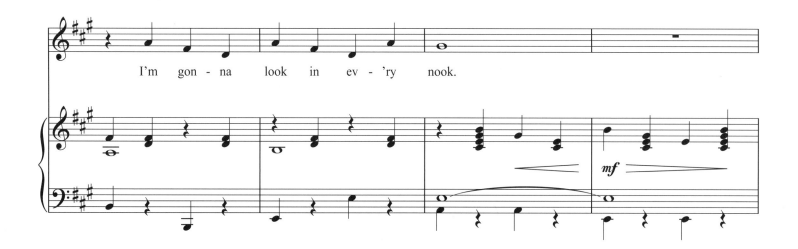

I'm gon - na look in ev - 'ry nook.

But how much long - er must I wait   With

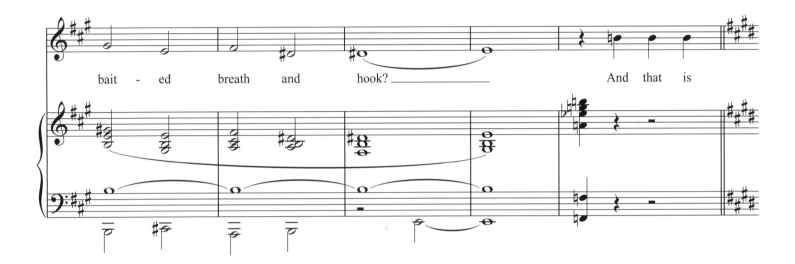

bait - ed breath and hook? _____   And that is

why, _____ though I'm pain-ful-ly shy, _____ I'm in-sane to know

Più mosso – Charleston beat

which sir? __ You, sir. __ Not you, sir. __ Then who, sir? __

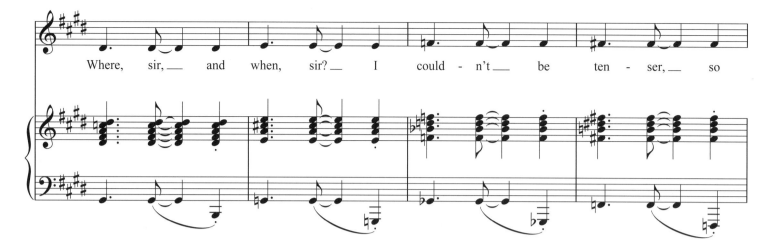

Where, sir,___ and when, sir?___ I could - n't___ be ten - ser,___ so

let's get ___ this done, man. ___ Get on with ___ the fun, man.

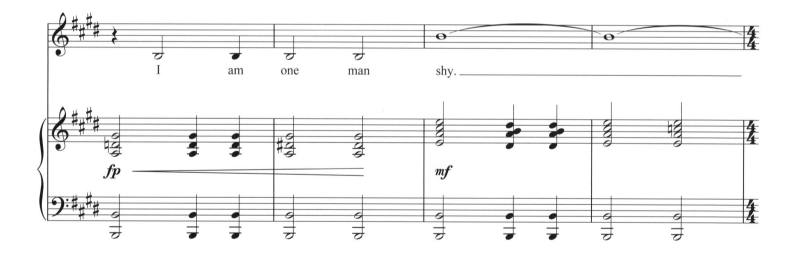

I am one man shy. _____

Jazz, in 4

THE SONG THAT GOES LIKE THIS

from MONTY PYTHON'S SPAMALOT

Lyrics by ERIC IDLE
Music by JOHN DU PREZ and ERIC IDLE

This song is a duet for the Lady of the Lake and Sir Dennis Galahad in the show, adapted here as a solo.

166

A sen-ti-men-tal song that casts a mag-ic spell. They

all will hum a-long. We'll o-ver-act like hell. Oh, this is the

song that goes like this.

Now we can go straight in-to the mid-dle eight, a bridge that is too

song that goes like this. _____ I

can't be-lieve there's more. It's far too long, I'm sure. That's the

_mp_

bring out L.H.

troub-le with this song, it goes on and on and on. For

this is our song that is too long.

SPECIAL
from the Broadway Musical AVENUE Q

Music and Lyrics by ROBERT LOPEZ
and JEFF MARX

*Possible cut to ** for auditions.*

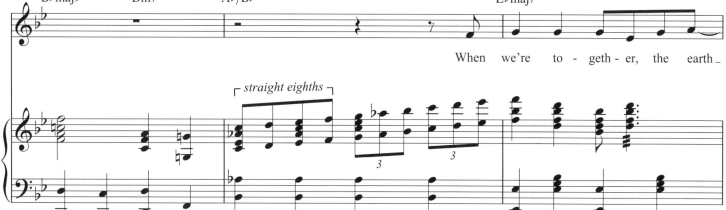

(spoken:) Yeah, they're real.

When we're to-geth-er, the earth _

will shake, _ and the stars will fall in - to the

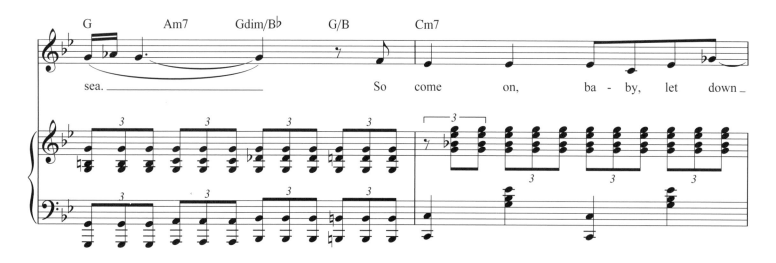

sea. _ So come on, ba - by, let down _

your guard. When your date's in the bath-room, I'll

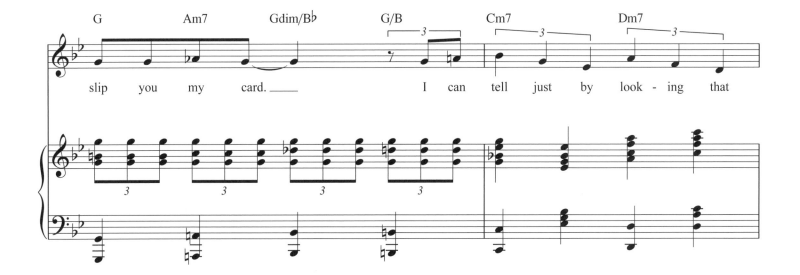

slip you my card. I can tell just by look-ing that

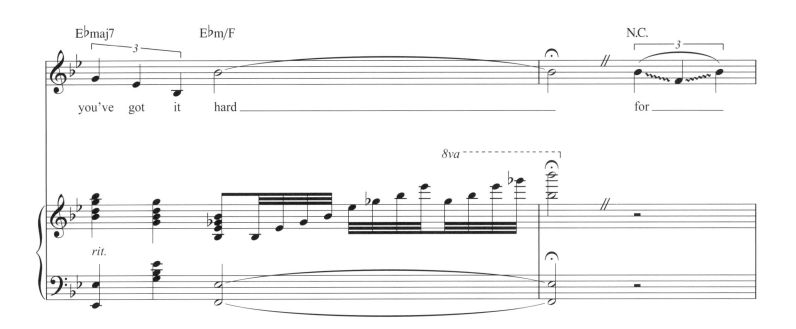

you've got it hard for

WHATEVER HAPPENED TO MY PART?

from MONTY PYTHON'S SPAMALOT

Lyrics by ERIC IDLE
Music by JOHN DU PREZ and ERIC IDLE

stage for far too long. It's ag - es since I had a

song. This is one un-hap-py di - va. The pro-

duc - ers have de - ceived her. There is noth - ing I can sing from my

heart. What-ev - er hap-pened to my part? I am

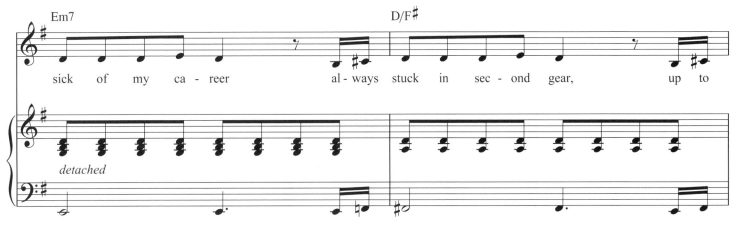

sick of my ca-reer al-ways stuck in sec-ond gear, up to

here with frus-tra-tion and with fears. I've no Gram-my, no re-wards. I've no

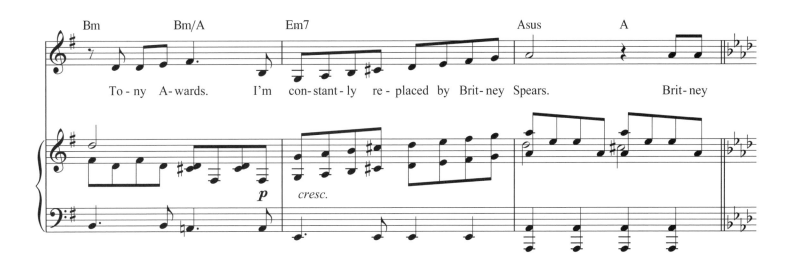

To-ny A-wards. I'm con-stant-ly re-placed by Brit-ney Spears. Brit-ney

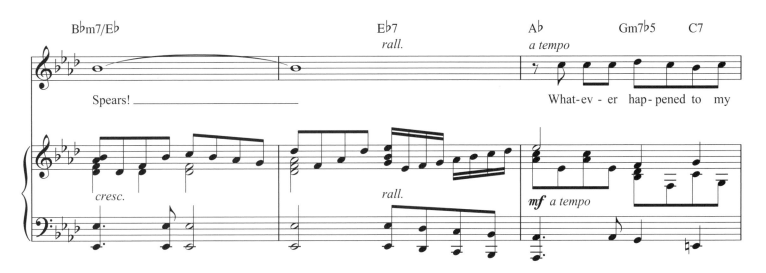

Spears! _____ What-ev-er hap-pened to my

show? I was a hit. Now, I don't know. __ I'm with a

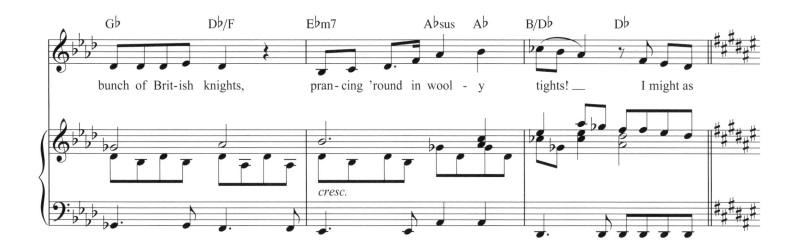

bunch of Brit-ish knights, pran-cing 'round in wool-y tights! __ I might as

well go __ to the pub. They've been out search - ing for a

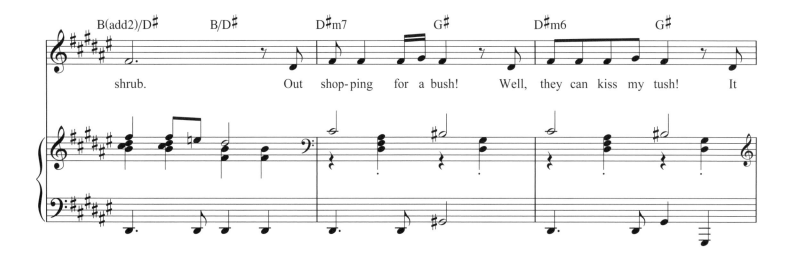

shrub. Out shop-ping for a bush! Well, they can kiss my tush! It

STEPSISTERS' LAMENT

from CINDERELLA

Lyrics by OSCAR HAMMERSTEIN II
Music by RICHARD RODGERS

Why would a fel-low want a girl like her, a frail and fluf - fy beau - ty?

Why can't a fel-low ev - er once pre-fer a sol - id girl like me? She's a froth - y lit - tle

In the show this song is sung by both sisters.

bub - ble _____ with a flim - sy kind of charm, _____ And with ver - y lit - tle

trou - ble _____ I could break her lit - tle arm! Oh, oh,

why would a fel - low want a girl like her, So ob - vious - ly un - u - sual?

Why can't a fel - low ev - er once pre - fer a u - sual girl like me? Her

cheeks are a pret-ty shade of pink, But not an-y pink-er than a rose is. Her

skin may be del-i-cate and soft, But not an-y soft-er than a doe's is. Her

neck is no whit-er than a swan's. She's on-ly as dain-ty as a dai-sy. She's

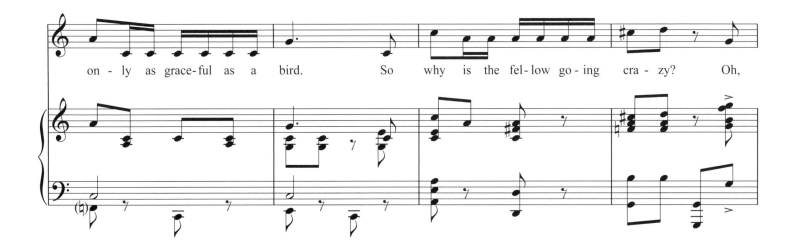

on-ly as grace-ful as a bird. So why is the fel-low go-ing cra-zy? Oh,

why would a fel - low want a girl like her, a girl who's mere - ly

love - ly? Why can't a fel - low ev - er once pre - fer a

girl who's mere - ly me? What's the mat - ter with the man? What's the mat - ter with the

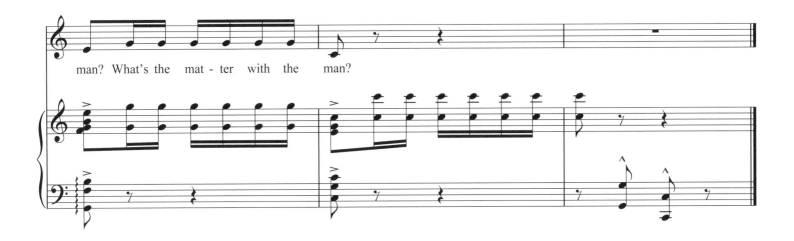

man? What's the mat - ter with the man?

TO KEEP MY LOVE ALIVE

from A CONNECTICUT YANKEE

Words by LORENZ HART
Music by RICHARD RODGERS

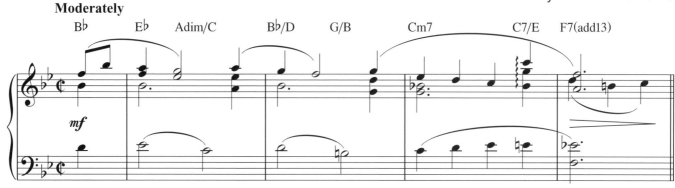

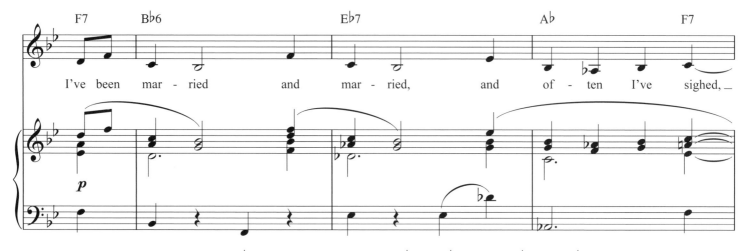

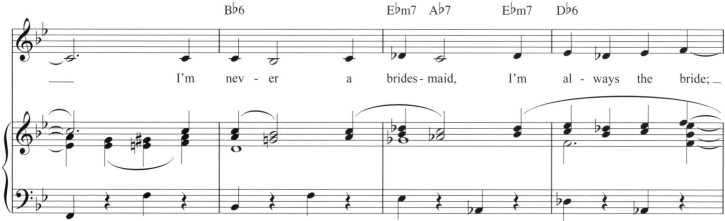

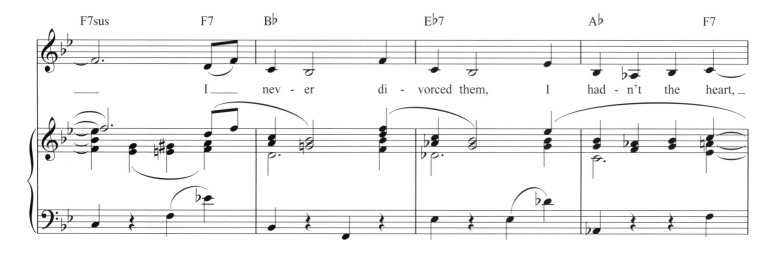

WHERE IS THE LIFE THAT LATE I LED?

from KISS ME, KATE

Words and Music by
COLE PORTER

Allegro con fuoco

PETRUCHIO:

Since I

reached _____ the charm - ing age of pu - ber - ty, _____ I be -

gan _____ to fin - ger fem - i - nine curls. _____ Like a

show _____ that's typ - i - cal - ly Shu - bert - y, _____ I have

al - ways had a mult - i - tude of girls. _____ But

much broader-ad lib., freely

now that a mar - ried man, _____ at last, am I, _____ How a -

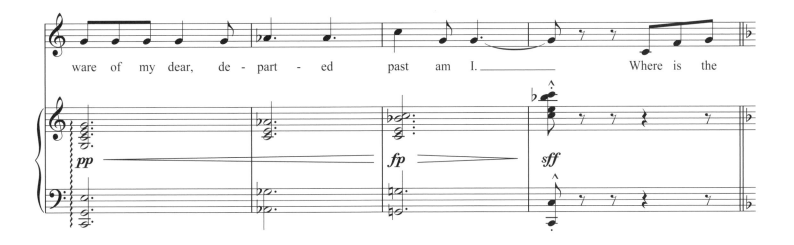

ware of my dear, de - part - ed past am I. _____ Where is the

[Moderate March Tempo]

life that late I _____ led? _____ Where is it

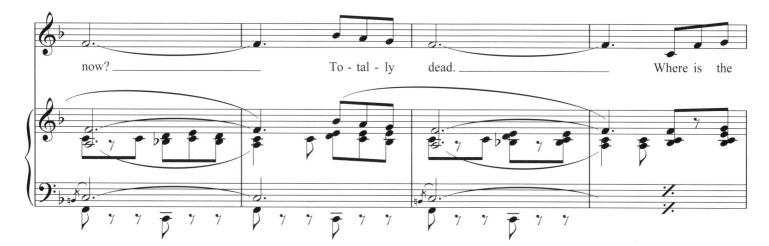

now? _____ To - tal - ly dead. _____ Where is the

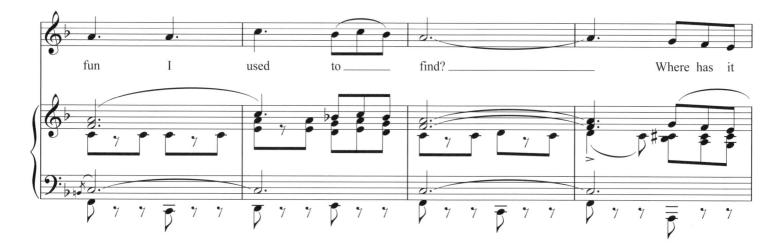

fun I used to _____ find? _____ Where has it

gone? _____ Gone with the wind. _____ A

mar - ried life _____ may all be well _____ But

rais - ing an heir Could nev - er com - pare With rais - ing a bit of

hell. So I re - peat what first I _____ said, _____

____ Where is the life that late I, In dear Mi -

[Andante lamentoso, rubato]

la - no,____ where are you, Mo - mo,____ Still sell-ing those pic - tures of the scrip - tures in the

[legato] *[rhythmically]*

Duo - mo?____ And *Ca - ro - li - na,____ Where are you **Li - na,____ Still ped - dling your

[legato]

piz - za in the streets o' Ta - or - mi - na?____ And in Fi - ren - ze,____ where are you,

[rhythmically] *[legato]* *p*

A - lice,____ Still there in your pret - ty, it - ty-bit - ty Pit - ti pal - ace?____ And sweet Luc-

rit.

[rhythmically] *rit.*

*Pronounced "Caroleena"   **"Leena"

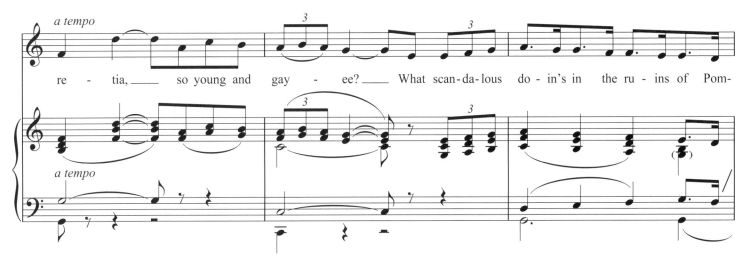

re - tia,_____ so young and gay - ee?_____ What scan-da-lous do - in's in the ru - ins of Pom-

[Moderate March Tempo]

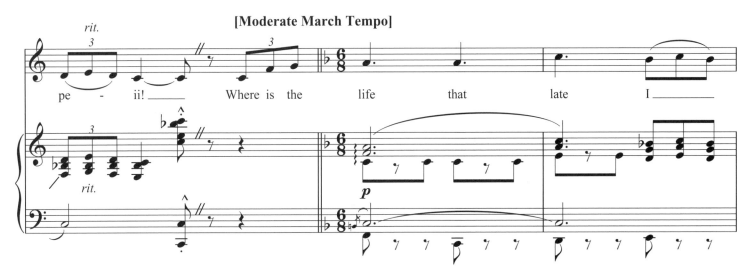

pe - ii!_____ Where is the life that late I_____

led?_____ Where is it now?_____ To - tal - ly

dead._____ Where is the fun I used to_____

find? _____ Where has it gone? _____ Gone with the

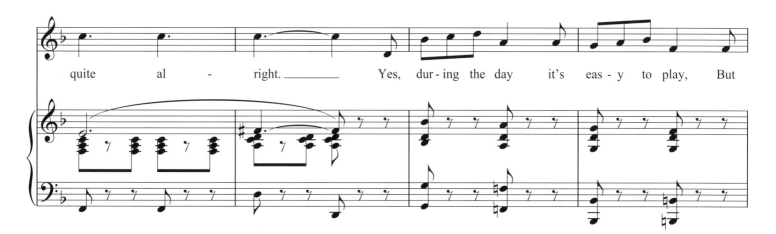

wind. _____ The mar - riage game _____ is

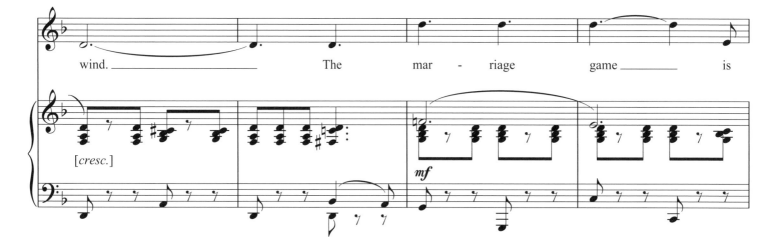

quite al - right. _____ Yes, dur-ing the day it's eas - y to play, But

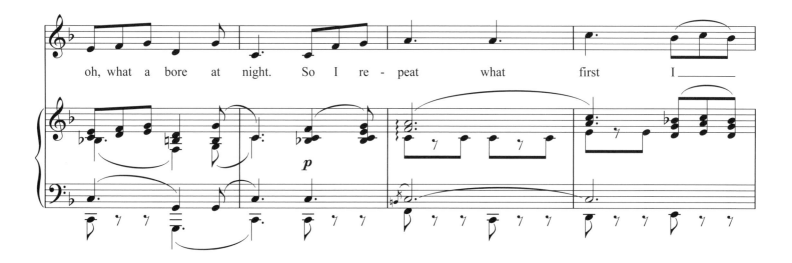

oh, what a bore at night. So I re - peat what first I _____

said: _____ Where is the life that

[Andante lamentoso, rubato]

late I Where is Re - bec - ca, ____ my Beck - i - weck - io? ____ Could still she be

p [*legato*]

cruis - ing that a - mus - ing Pon - te Vecch - io? ____ Where is Fe - do - ra, ____ The wild vi -

[*rhythmically*] [*legato*]

ra - go? ____ It's luck - y I missed her gang - ster sis - ter from Chi - ca - go. ____ Where is Ve -

[*rhythmically*]

ne - tia,___ who loved to chat so?___ Could still she be drink - in' in her stink - in' pink pa-

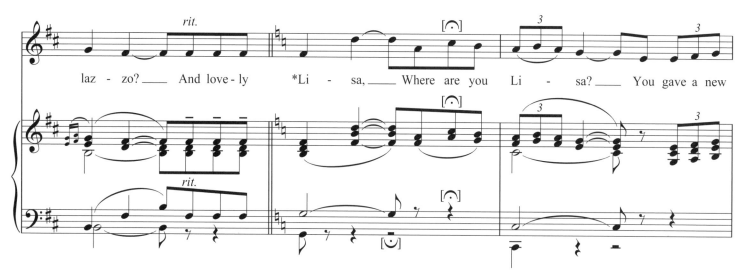

laz - zo?___ And love - ly *Li - sa,___ Where are you Li - sa?___ You gave a new

[Moderate March Tempo]

mean - ing to the lean - ing tow'r of Pi - za!___ Where is the life that

late I___ led?_____ Where is it now?_____

*Pronounced "Leeza"

To - tal - ly dead. _____ Where is the fun I

used to _____ find? _____ Where has it gone? _____

_____ Gone with the wind. _____ I've oft' been told _____ of

ff   fz   mf

nup - tial bliss, _____ But what do you do, at quar - ter to two, With

ad lib., freely

p colla voce

a tempo

on - ly a shrew to kiss? So I re - peat what first I _____ said: _____

ad lib., freely

_____ Where is the life that late _____ I _____

led? _____

YOU'LL BE BACK

from HAMILTON

Words and Music by
LIN-MANUEL MIRANDA

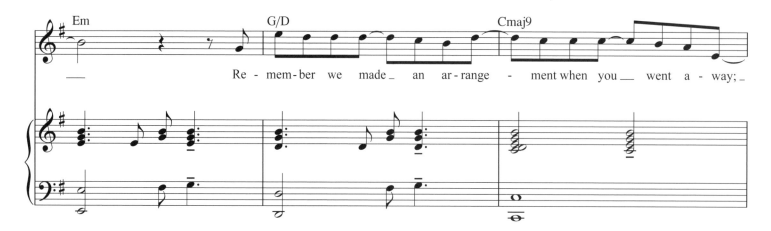

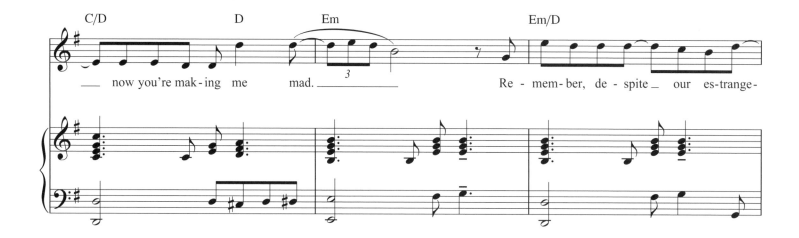

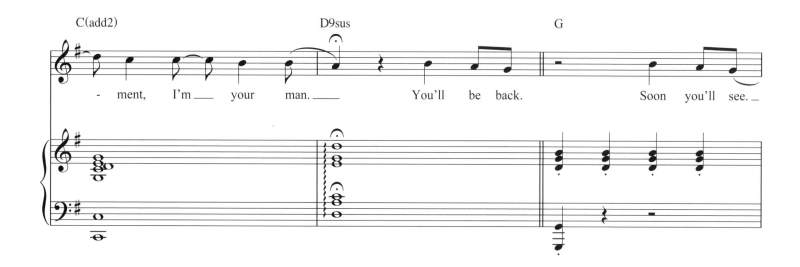

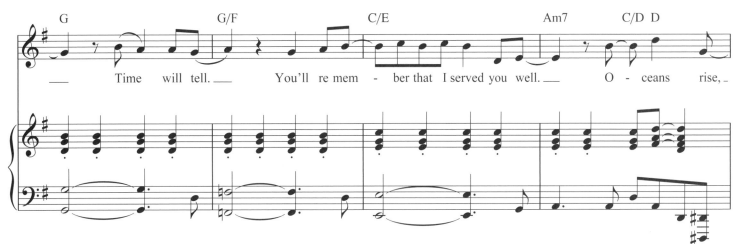

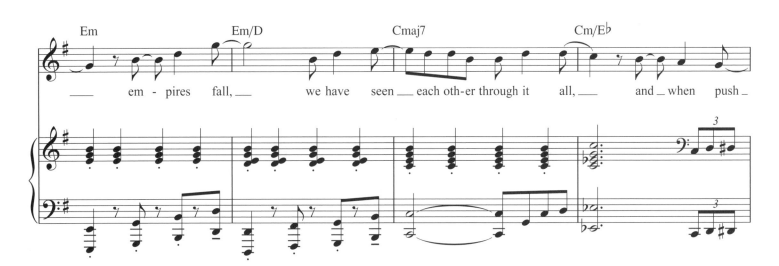

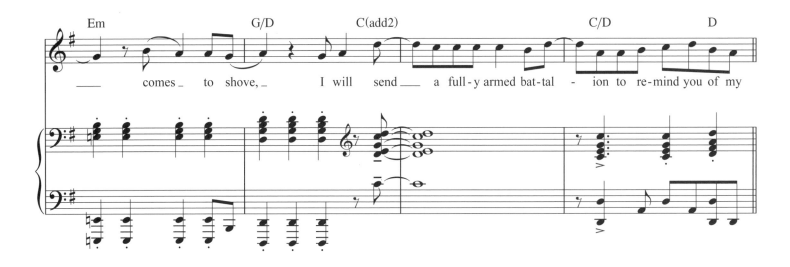

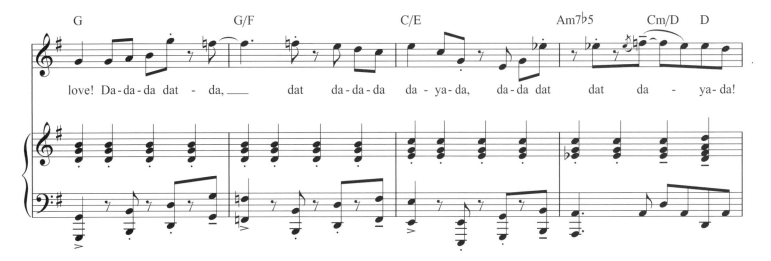

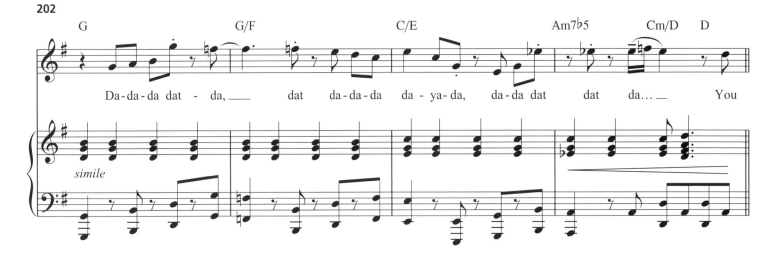

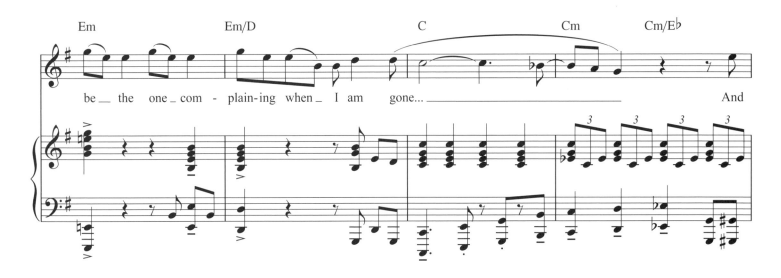

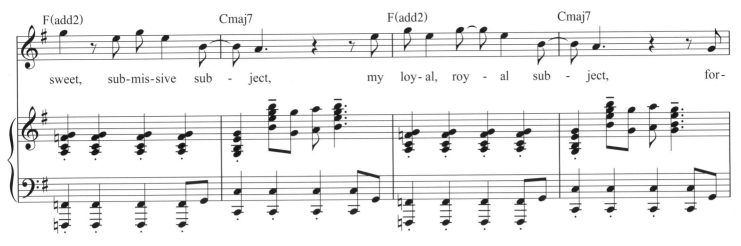

sweet, sub-mis-sive sub - ject, my loy-al, roy-al sub - ject, for-

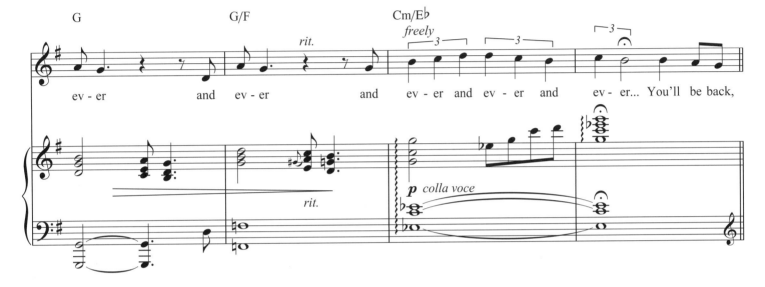

ev-er and ev-er and ev-er and ev-er and ev-er... You'll be back,

like be-fore. I will fight the fight and win the war for your love,

for your praise, and I'll love you till my dy-ing days. When you're gone

I'll __ go mad, __ so __ don't throw __ a-way this thing we had. __ 'Cause __ when push __

__ comes __ to shove, __ I will kill __ your friends and fam-'ly __ to re-mind you of __ my love. __

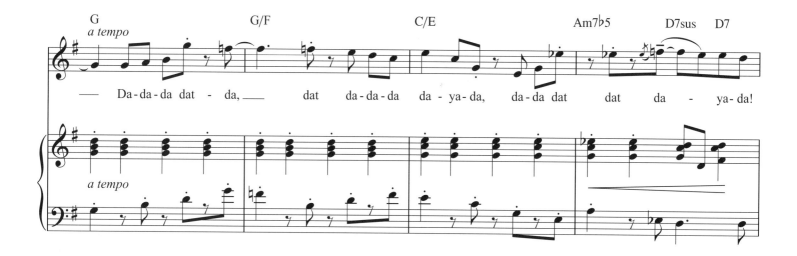

__ Da-da-da dat - da, __ dat da-da-da da - ya - da, da-da dat dat da - ya - da!

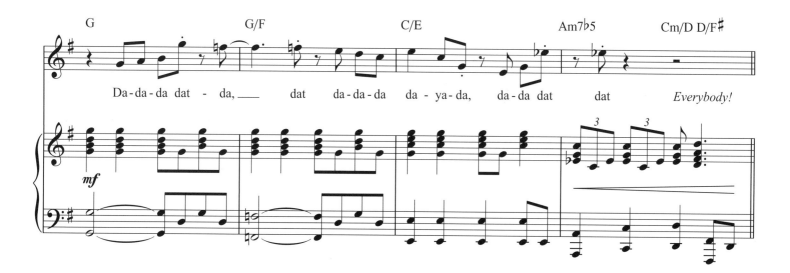

Da-da-da dat - da, __ dat da-da-da da - ya - da, da-da dat dat *Everybody!*

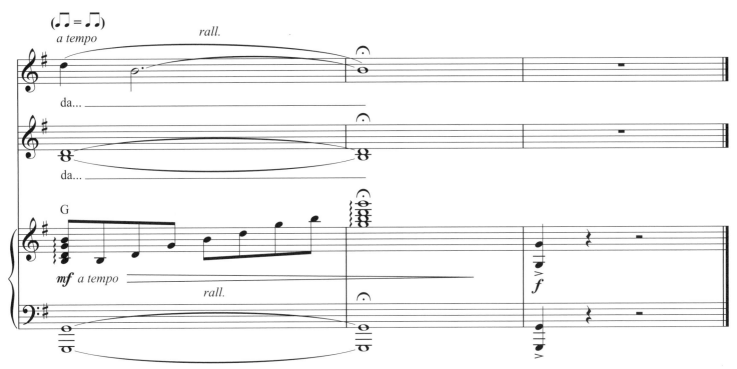

YOU WON'T SUCCEED ON BROADWAY

from MONTY PYTHON'S SPAMALOT

Lyrics by ERIC IDLE
Music by JOHN DU PREZ and ERIC IDLE

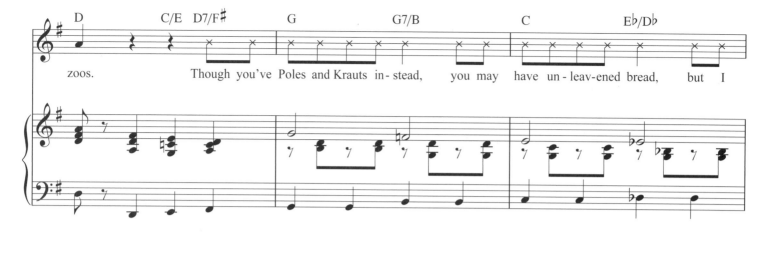

zoos. Though you've Poles and Krauts in-stead, you may have un-leav-ened bread, but I

tell you, you are dead if you don't have an - y Jews.

They

won't care if it's wit-ty, or ev -'ry-thing looks pret-ty. They'll sim-ply say it's shit-ty, and re-

fuse. No - bod-y will go, sir, if it's not ko - sher, then no show, sir. E - ven

goy - im won't be dim e - nough to choose. Put on shows that make men stare, with lots of

girls in un - der - wear. You may e - ven have the fin - est of re - views. But the

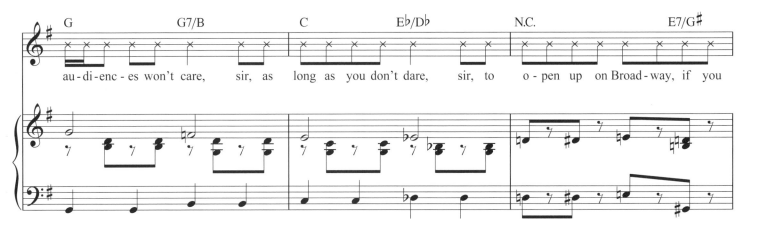

au - di - enc - es won't care, sir, as long as you don't dare, sir, to o - pen up on Broad - way, if you

don't have an - y Jews.

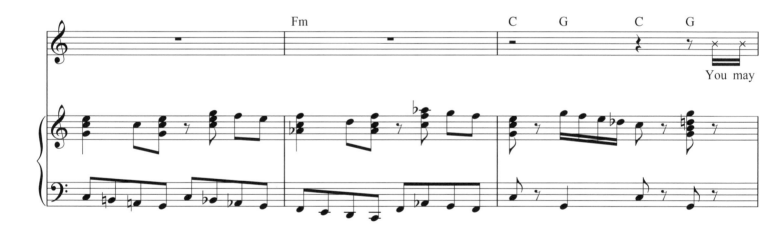

You may

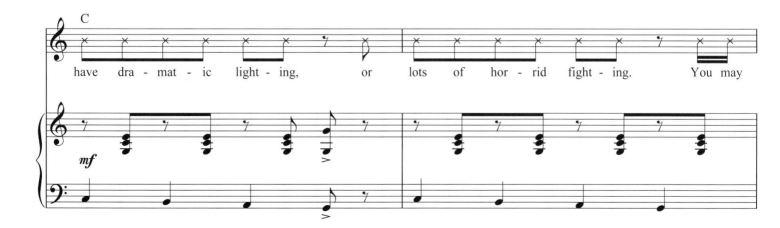

have dra - mat - ic light - ing, or lots of hor - rid fight - ing. You may

bring on a pi-an-o, but they will not give a damn-o if you don't have an-y Jews.

Looney Tunes

Hey!

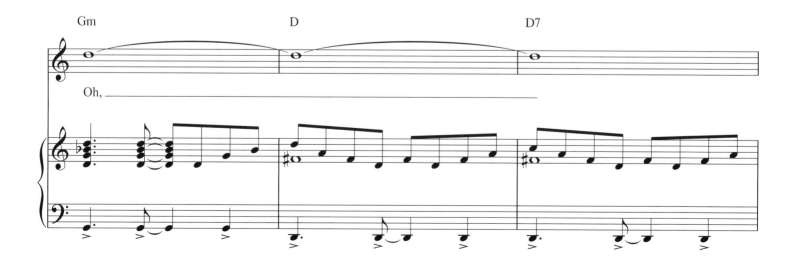

Oh, _____

oy! You may fill your plays with gays, have Ni - ger - i - an girls in stays. You may

e - ven have some shik - sas mak - ing stews. You have - n't got a clue, if

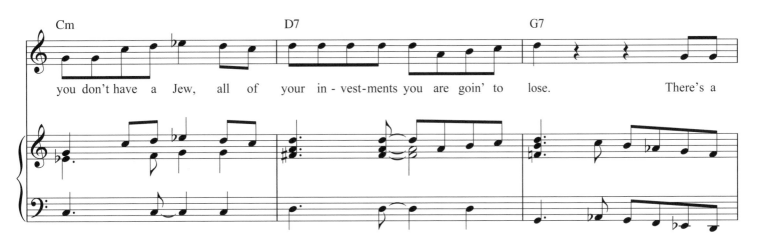

you don't have a Jew, all of your in - vest - ments you are goin' to lose. There's a

ver - y small per - cen - tile who en - joys a danc - ing gen - tile. I'm sad to be the one with this bad

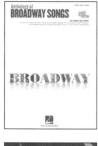

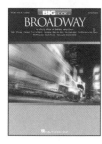